90 DAY
BIBLE READING
CHALLENGE

Books by Mary DeMuth

FROM BAKER PUBLISHING GROUP

*The Day I Met Jesus**
Worth Living
Love, Pray, Listen
90-Day Bible Reading Challenge

** with Frank Viola*

90 DAY
BIBLE READING
CHALLENGE

Read the Whole Bible,
Change Your Whole Life

MARY DEMUTH

BETHANYHOUSE
a division of Baker Publishing Group
Minneapolis, Minnesota

Published by Bethany House Publishers
Minneapolis, Minnesota
www.bethanyhouse.com

Bethany House Publishers is a division of
Baker Publishing Group, Grand Rapids, Michigan

Printed in the United States of America

ISBN 978-0-7642-4204-5 (paper)
ISBN 978-1-4934-4396-3 (ebook)
ISBN 978-0-7642-4237-3 (casebound)

Library of Congress Cataloging-in-Publication Control Number: 2023012860

Unless otherwise indicated, Scripture quotations are taken from the Holy Bible, New Living Translation, copyright © 1996, 2004, 2015 by Tyndale House Foundation. Used by permission of Tyndale House Publishers, Inc., Carol Stream, Illinois 60188. All rights reserved.

Scripture quotation from the Amplified® Bible (AMPC), copyright © 1954, 1958, 1962, 1964, 1965, 1987 by The Lockman Foundation. Used by permission. www.Lockman.org

Scripture quotations identified ESV are from The Holy Bible, English Standard Version® (ESV®), copyright © 2001 by Crossway, a publishing ministry of Good News Publishers. Used by permission. All rights reserved. ESV Text Edition: 2016

Scripture quotations identified NASB are from the (NASB®) New American Standard Bible®, Copyright © 1960, 1971, 1977, 1995 by The Lockman Foundation. Used by permission. All rights reserved. www.lockman.org

Scripture quotation from The New Testament in Modern English by J. B. Phillips copyright © 1960, 1972 J. B. Phillips. Administered by The Archbishops' Council of the Church of England. Used by Permission.

Published in association with Books & Such Literary Management, www.booksand such.com.

Baker Publishing Group publications use paper produced from sustainable forestry practices and post-consumer waste whenever possible.

23 24 25 26 27 28 29   7 6 5 4 3 2 1

To my husband, Patrick,
and his theological hero, N. T. Wright:
Thank you for deeply influencing my heart
in writing this book.

To my friend Ellen Harbin,
who loves, absorbs, and teaches
the Word of God with vigor.

CONTENTS

Contents

Contents

INTRODUCTION

I've had two types of racing experiences in my life—the longer slog of a half marathon and a shorter race called a sprint triathlon. Each needed specific kinds of skills.

For the half marathon, I focused my training on endurance, on putting footfall after footfall on the pavement without stopping. I had to cultivate lung endurance, to keep my breathing steady over the long haul. I had to be cautious of shin splints from overuse. And I needed to concentrate on fuel while I ran. (I used to eat gummies made of honey to keep me going!) Honestly, I didn't know if I would ever finish that race. The last three miles stretched longer than I anticipated. Joy came when I finished, but pain followed me as I limped to the car.

The sprint was an entirely different experience. I had to practice my transitions between swimming and biking, then biking to running, trying to shave seconds off my time. The distances were shorter than longer triathlons, so pacing throughout was faster. I had to work on consistency and cadence. But in finishing the triathlon, I felt invigorated—ready to take on the next race adventure.

I want to invite you on a similar (yet not as physically taxing) adventure—one that you've most likely never experienced before—at least not in the timeframe I'm proposing. It's more sprint than marathon.

Let me back up a bit.

A couple of years ago, I felt dry in my Bible reading. I'd read through the Bible several times, utilizing one of those one-year Bibles. I varied it between reading straight through a normal Bible and reading a chronological Bible. Like many, I got a bit bogged down in places, particularly through Ezekiel. Even so, I was glad I did it. I wanted to be able to say I had read the entire Bible, though the experience felt a bit disjointed.

Enter *brisk reading*. I'm not sure where I first saw the concept, though my friend Keith Ferrin has spoken and written about it before. But I'm pretty sure it coincided with a deepening distaste for how often I found myself phone-gazing each day. So much phone. So little truth. I found myself slipping into guilt and despair the more I absorbed the world's so-called wisdom. How could I counterbalance all that scrolling?

What if I were as intensely focused on my Bible as I had been on my phone screen? Could I read the Bible in a couple months? Could that reset my obsession with searching for something interesting on my phone each day?

I opened my Bible to its last page where Revelation 22:21 concludes the Word of God (in my case, page 2199) and divided it by the number of days in which I wanted to read the Bible. That gave me the number of pages I needed to read each day. Each reading would take a chunk of time, but I'd spend less time doom-scrolling and more time reading who begat whom and what shenanigans the nation of Israel was up to—at least while I waded through the Old Testament.

I assumed I would get bored. Who wouldn't?

I thought such a quick read of the Word of God wouldn't change me—much.

I was wrong.

Not only did I *not* get bored, but my fascination level grew with each daily reading session. I looked forward to immersing myself in the ever-changing landscape of the Bible. I didn't have time to dwell—although that was something I also had found deeply rewarding and valuable. In this brisk-reading endeavor, I simply kept reading while the story of Scripture unfolded before me like the best epic cinema. At times, I took notes so I could revisit portions of Scripture later. But often I just absorbed and made connections.

The connections I'd missed by reading more slowly became obvious. The message of the Bible leapt from its pages, grabbing me, wooing me into the story. I often asked myself, "How would I feel if this were happening to me?" This kind of question helped me finally realize that the Bible wasn't merely words stitched together to proclaim truth. It was chock-full of breathing, very real human beings who intersected in God's grand narrative. These people moved from characters on a page to people I might want to have lunch with—or not (hello, Nabal).

And oh, how I fell in love with the messy folks populating the pages of the Bible! I realized I was not alone in my penchant for choosing myself first. Even when people royally messed up, God's plan continued forward, always advancing despite the foibles of clay-footed humanity. In short, I realized that I cannot thwart the will of God. I'm certainly not powerful enough.

In addition, I constantly ran into what The Bible Project calls "hyperlinks"—those Easter eggs of Scripture woven throughout the pages. That seemingly random place connected to that Old Testament saint saying those words in Hebrew that echoed in the Apostle Paul's Greek poem.

Instead of reading the Bible with questions in mind, asking it to solve hermeneutical conundrums, I read it plainly, allowing it to unfold before me like a well-told story around a campfire.

Without much effort (other than setting aside daily time), I became a better and more joyful student of the Word of God. That, in turn, translated into the way I taught the Bible—holistically. No longer was God the angry deity in the Old Testament, the hippie feel-good deity of the New Testament, or the *woo-woo* Holy

Spirit permeating the whole Bible. This Trinity was irresistible, ever opening my eyes to the great redemptive story of humanity.

I could nearly feel the anguish of God the Father lamenting over the waywardness of his children, the nation of Israel. It was easy to grow angry that he afforded them more and more and more grace. He truly was the God of the umpteenth chance. Reading briskly revealed that future redemption was hinted at through Law, poetry, and prophetic utterances. I began to understand the grief of humanity, that it was acceptable to cry and lament, and how God intersected that grief.

As a storyteller, I appreciated the narrative structure of the Bible, from setting the story world (creation, Eden), to inciting incident (Satan and the fall of humanity), to conflicts aplenty (Israel's formation, kingdom, and exile, and the remnant's return), to the climax (Jesus's life, death, resurrection, and inauguration of the church), to the *denouement* where we live and breathe today. But even though Scripture walks us through this story arc, there is a higher climax still—the glittering New Heavens and New Earth, where everything will finally be made whole and right, permeated by God's great *shalom*.

Those two months briskly reading through the Word of God changed my life. In the past several decades, I've grown through discipleship, mission, and Bible study. But I can honestly say my deepest, most profound growth has come through this simple practice of brisk reading. Whenever I teach the Bible, I tell others about this secret and encourage them to take up the challenge. I have taught my Life Group at church to do the same. And I've led others through the practice and had the privilege of watching God utterly change lives through the brisk reading of Scripture. My passion for biblical literacy has infused my journey alongside others, and now I have taken all that goodness and curated it in the book you're holding in your hands.

It can happen for you, too, over the course of ninety days. I hope you can sense my excitement for you as you embark on this journey.

Confident that you, too, are pressed for time, I've divided the Bible into ninety daily readings, chronologically. You're provided something to ponder each day to help you navigate the reading. I'll be there to encourage you along the way because I know the fruit that will come in your life as a result.

If it works better for your life's pace and daily rhythms, I've divided each day into three readings. You can choose to do them all at once, then consider the insights gleaned, or you can take bites throughout the day, perhaps morning, noon, and night. The way you choose to read the Word of God at a brisk pace for this challenge is up to you.

An additional admonition: You may want to find a text-only, readable version of the Bible. A study Bible's notes and devotions may distract you from brisk reading. When I told my husband about this book, he said, "I'd have a hard time just reading the Bible. I'd get stuck on an idea and want to explore it." Having a text-only Bible (or even listening to the Bible) will help you keep moving forward.

You also don't have to "read" through the Bible each day. Instead, consider listening to the chapters as you take a walk or do the dishes or drive to work. Hearing the Word of God is a practical yet powerful way to ingest larger portions of Scripture.

Here's what I've learned as I devoured the Bible: This practice will instigate a life reset.

We've been battered by the world. We've sunk into cynicism and despair. We've let the wisdom of our age inform our worth, what we think about, and our joy (or lack of it). In short, we've saturated ourselves in the fickle ways of humankind. According to Paul, we've "traded the truth about God for a lie" (Romans 1:25), allowing the kingdoms of this world to influence our perspective. Paul continues with a stern caution in the same verse, "So they worshiped and served the things God created instead of the Creator himself, who is worthy of eternal praise! Amen."

Reading the Bible in three months will help you wrest yourself away from the siren call of the world so you can stop worshiping the opinions of others and reorient your heart to worship the One who died for you.

This is a significant leap, an important investment in the next years of your walk with Jesus. It's a choice to give your future self an incredible gift—the gift of wisdom and a settled knowledge of the Word of God.

As you read the Bible briskly, ask yourself these questions: When people and creation are not functioning properly, when they are not *tov* (the Hebrew word for good), how does God respond? How does he feel? Have you considered that God knows grief?

- Did he grieve when he discovered Adam and Eve hiding in the garden?
- Did he grieve when he had to banish them from Eden?
- Did he grieve when Cain murdered his brother without provocation?
- Did he grieve when violence covered the earth, inviting his flood of judgment? You can nearly hear the lament as you read these words: "The LORD observed the extent of human wickedness on the earth, and he saw that everything they thought or imagined was consistently and totally evil. So the LORD was sorry he had ever made them and put them on the earth. *It broke his heart*" (Genesis 6:5–6, emphasis mine).
- Did he grieve as people attempted to become like him, building a tower to the sky?

As you rapidly go through the Bible, your reading will deepen if you see it through the lens of the grief of God. God processes his grief through the pages of Scripture, yet even in pain, his heart always bends toward redemption. You see it in the shedding of blood, covering Adam and Eve with skins for protection. Even in his grief, he turned toward humanity and made promises he would keep.

One of the most powerful practices I've implemented in a brisk reading of the Bible has simply been to ask the question: How would that make me feel? Whether I was reading about Eve, who took that first bite of forbidden fruit, or wondering about how Adam must have felt when his son bled into the earth or how Noah's nameless wife experienced life on a boat, I asked myself, *How would I feel if that were me?* This simple exercise places me squarely in the story and helps me remember that these people are not characters in a novel; they were living, breathing human beings who felt, broke promises, worried, hid, and attempted to love.

Many books ask you to fast certain things for periods of time in order to reset your metabolism or will. People are encouraged to take healing journeys in quarterly increments. But this book is a ninety-day reset for spiritual health, a feeding of your soul. The only thing this reset will cost you is your time.

Reading the Bible in ninety days will be time well spent. You'll be able to look back on your life before this brisk-reading experiment and call it "before." The "after" will be a transformed you, better attuned to the very Spirit of God, in love with the Scriptures penned by his hand.

Before we begin, how would you answer these questions?

- Do you want to grow?
- Do you long to be restored?
- Have you lost interest in the Bible?
- Does your spiritual life feel stagnant?
- Are you battling cynicism or excessive worry?
- Do you sense something's missing, but can't put your finger on it?
- Have you found yourself drifting?
- Has your passion for Jesus ebbed?
- Are you tangled up by the words of Bible teachers, unsure if they're teaching truth?

- Are you wrestling doubts?
- Have you always wanted to read the Bible all the way through but were scared?
- Do you have a friend or family member who might want to do this with you?
- Are you ready for transformation from the inside out?

If you answered yes to any of these questions, welcome to the adventure of brisk Bible reading! For the next ninety days, you'll experience more of the Bible than you ever have before in a concentrated period of time.

How to Take the Challenge

All you'll need for this challenge is a time slot of about an hour a day (broken up in three segments, if you choose), this book, and a pen, if you're prone to write in your Bible. Whether you read the Bible passage before you pick up this book or after, the experience will be the same. You'll gain insight about what you've read either way.

Each daily passage will bring surprising illumination, as well as give the encouragement you need every day. There's no need for my summarizing what you've read, but I'll be pulling out nuggets of wisdom to chew on. Whether you begin in the morning, read the Bible at night or all through the day, or listen to it on your way to and from work, you'll have truths to digest, with an expansion of the text and pep talks to keep you going. Consider each day's entry as if it's a letter from a friend who's walked that pathway before you.

- We'll begin with the Creation and Fall of humankind.
- Then we'll move on to the time of Abraham and the covenant God made with him to bless the whole world through his offspring.

- Next, we'll look at the exodus—a pivotal story in the narrative of Scripture. (Aside: My theologically trained husband, Patrick, believes you can't read the book of Romans unless you've read it through the lens of the exodus.)
- Then we'll walk through the covenant God made with the people of Israel from Mount Sinai, where he delivers the Ten Commandments twice.
- Afterward, we'll wander the wilderness with the rebellious Israelites.
- Finally, we'll make our way to the Promised Land.
- We'll cover the rise and fall of the kingdom of Israel.
- Then we'll read the prophets who prophesied before the exile of Israel.
- This will be followed by all those rich wisdom books of the Bible.
- Next, we'll read from all the prophets who were active during the exile of Israel.
- We'll return from exile with the Israelites in Ezra, Nehemiah, and Esther.
- We'll read prophets who also prophesied after the exile.
- Then we'll reread the story of Israel to summarize the Old Testament through 1 and 2 Chronicles.
- At last, we'll tackle Jesus and the kingdom of God in the Gospels.
- Then we'll explore what it looks like to be the church on earth through the writings of Paul, James, Peter, John, and the author of Hebrews.
- Of course, we'll end with the book of Revelation. (Do you see that we begin in a garden in Genesis, and end in a city in Revelation?)
- And, to offer you devotional Scripture throughout your journey, every day you'll read a psalm or two!

Friend, are you ready to be a brisk reader of the Bible? Have you set aside your time, grabbed your Bible (or your earbuds), and asked the Lord to prepare you for this adventure? Mind if I pray for you as we begin?

> *Lord Jesus, would you prepare the heart of my friend for the absolute joy of discovery awaiting them? I pray you'll settle any fears, quiet any antagonistic voices, and renew my friend's mind today. Would you absolutely change their heart and perspective as they take on this rigorous but redemptive task? Be very near to my friend. Speak life over them as they read. Quicken them to be attentive to the still, small voice of your Spirit. Bring unexplainable joy as they dive into your beautiful word, I pray. Amen.*

GOD MADE EVERYTHING

- ○ **Morning:** Genesis 1–7
- ○ **Noon:** Genesis 8–15
- ○ **Night:** Psalms 1–2

The story of us opens with "In the beginning God" (Genesis 1:1). Before anything else existed—including time—God lived in community as the Trinity—God the Father, God the Son, God the Holy Spirit. The divine dance was itself a relationship, and this particular relationship longed to create something tangible from that love, similar to how some married couples long for children.

God's beautiful desire culminated through language. He spoke the heavens and the earth into existence, something substantive out of chaotic nothingness. He made every creature that crawled, swam, and flew. God's crowning achievement was people—particularly Adam and Eve. Unlike the animals who had no will, Adam and Eve bore his image and were given important responsibility to tame the creatures and tend the ground in a garden called Eden.

In that place there existed what the Hebrew Bible calls *tov*—goodness. In our world, we strip *good* of its ancient meaning. We call a rich cup of coffee good, but in the opening story of Genesis, this *good* means to have function, a universe running as it should.

So, when Satan broke into the revelry of *tov* in the form of a serpent, he introduced the word *ra,* which in its simplest form translates as *evil*. But there is more nuance. *Ra* is *tov*'s opposite. It means to be dysfunctional. Satan may have promised function through knowledge, but he delivered chaos through rebellion. Humanity listened to his smooth, slick words, then rebelled toward *ra*, and God brought consequences. What was once idyllic now became forbidden.

Ever since, dysfunction has been our lot. Do you relate?

Even so, our surprising Creator longed for relationship with his dysfunctional creation. He made a covenant (agreement) with Noah—signed by a rainbow in the sky—that he would never flood the earth again after humanity had descended into violent chaos. And then he continued to pursue his people by enacting a different covenant with Abram. God's heart, spilled onto the pages of Scripture, is that everyone would meet him, that all would be blessed, that all would return to *tov*.

In today's reading, you see the cycle of sin and redemption: All is good. Humankind sins. God grieves. He rescues. Repeat. God's plan, we learn, cannot be thwarted by us. He loves to rescue his people, even when we're being obstinate. That's *tov* news.

Lord, thank you for being tov, *even when I'm not. Forgive me for grieving your heart. Would you open my eyes to how you feel about this earth and your people? I long to be made whole again, to be beautifully functional in my daily life. Rescue me, I pray. Amen.*

GOD SEES YOU

○ **Morning:** Genesis 16–22
○ **Noon:** Genesis 23–28
○ **Night:** Psalm 3

In Genesis 16:8 the Angel of the Lord asks Sarai's handmaiden Hagar, "Where have you come from, and where are you going?"

Hagar stood there, bereft of hope, pregnant, amid the wilderness with nowhere to go.

"I'm running away from my mistress, Sarai," she replied.

Take note that she answered the first question, but not the second. It's a theme in today's reading, this journeying away from what was and a stepping out in faith toward what is next.

Hagar there named God *El-roi*, "the God who sees me" (Genesis 16:13). And the One who saw her instructed her to return to her difficult situation.

While it is true that sometimes God sends us backward to learn something about his care and character, it is also true that he compels us forward toward a new vision of what the world could be. And, surprisingly, he uses the most unobvious people to accomplish his kingdom purposes in this life.

Consider Abram and Sarai, a barren couple promised a child who would birth a nation whose borders included Canaan—where Abraham buried Sarah as a down payment of what was to come.

Consider Isaac, who received the same covenant even though his firstborn was cheated of his birthright.

Consider Jacob, who took that birthright and was taken advantage of by a cruel relative.

Things did not look promising for God's promises of a large nation or a landing place for that nation. Those he chose were clay-footed, broken, and needy.

And yet, they stumbled forward, and God kept his amazing promise to each generation. There is hope for all of us in that reality. God isn't looking for people of perfection to carry out his perfect plan. He is looking for folks who exercise faith, believe him, and take the next step toward an unknown but beautiful future.

Where you came from matters. It's the foundation of who you are today. And God is using all the past pain of your story to produce the kind of character that has the guts to trust God for where you are going. You may not be able to perceive it. Like the people in today's reading, you may feel barren or defeated or used. But God's purposes will prevail. Trusting him amid your current feelings is a marker of faith. Persevere!

> *Lord, I'm struggling. My past sometimes haunts me, and I don't even want to look back there. But you promise to use that past to prepare me for the future. Help me to trust you for what is next. I don't want to shrink from taking the next step. Amen.*

✓ Day 3

GOD CREATES FAMILIES

○ **Morning:** Genesis 29–35
○ **Noon:** Genesis 36–40
○ **Night:** Psalm 4

Today we see the formulation of the twelve tribes of Israel through Jacob's two wives, Leah and Rachel, and those two wives' servants, Zilpah and Bilhah. Leah birthed Reuben, Simeon, Levi, Judah, Issachar, and Zebulun. Her maidservant Zilpah had Gad and Asher. Rachel birthed Joseph and Benjamin (in childbirth with Benjamin, Rachel died). Her maidservant Bilhah had Dan and Naphtali. Together these sons would become Israel, first a people displaced, then a people homed in Palestine.

None of this was easy. None of this was clean.

Four women ached—an unloved one, a barren one, and two women offered to Jacob who were not his wife, which brought its own kind of grief. And above them all, Laban, a cruel taskmaster intent on squeezing every bit of wealth from his son-in-law and daughters. And yet, God's purposes prevail, even in the tangled mess of relationships, jealousies, and strife.

As Jacob (now renamed Israel, which means "God contended"[1]) fathered his children and watched them grow, strife evolved afresh. In Genesis 37, you read about Joseph entering the scene, a dreamer in the midst of contentious brothers. True to form (they are the progeny of the one who contended with God), they connived to murder their dreamer brother, then settled on murdering his future instead, selling him into slavery.

You can almost hear the movie track's cadence shift from triumph to minor tone at this moment. Twelve tribes essentially become eleven, while Israel mourns and mourns and mourns.

All seems lost.

But all is not.

Tomorrow you'll see deliverance in the most surprising, unusual way. Today you watched Joseph's faithfulness in persecution, and his desire for integrity put to the test. His is not merely the story of the future rescue of a famished people—it is our story too. Like Joseph and the women of this story, we are broken and sometimes consumed with grief. Evil seems to win. Betrayal becomes our lot. We suffer under the weight of other people's desire for power. We are maligned, wrongly accused, and assigned impure motives.

Yet, like Joseph in Potiphar's house, we have a choice.

Like Joseph wrongfully imprisoned, we have a choice.

Like the women of Israel, we have a choice.

The choice to believe God is holy and worthy of our obedience. To trust in God's ability to deliver, rather than in our ability to fix everything. To walk with integrity even when those around us would rather entice us to sin. Like Joseph, we can say to those tempting us, "How could I do such a wicked thing? It would be a great sin against God" (Genesis 39:9).

Lord, the story of your nation is painful. So many wounds! I understand it's because people are broken and sin-bent. I am broken and sin-bent too. But oh, how I long to be like Joseph, full of integrity, particularly when I'm hurting or being maligned. Birth in me a Joseph-like steadfastness and faithfulness today, I pray. Amen.

✓ Day 4

GOD ELEVATES THE IMPRISONED

- ○ **Morning:** Genesis 41–45
- ○ **Noon:** Genesis 46–50
- ○ **Night:** Psalms 5–6

You've made it to the fourth day! By now I hope you're beginning to see how reading a large portion of Scripture daily helps you truly understand the grand narrative of the Bible. Today we take a deep dive into the life of Joseph, one of Israel's twelve sons, who seems to have a separate story from his brothers until everything converges in a series of dynamic scenes.

And what scenes those are! Accusations of stealing. Seemingly unrealistic demands. Exasperation to the brink of despair on the part of Joseph's brothers. All culminating in the big reveal—the brother they sold into slavery became their ticket to emancipation.

This reminds us that God can use the direst of circumstances to bring about his purposes. And this: Our integrity in the quiet places matters.

You see the playing out of this in Genesis 49, where Israel blesses his children. He does not hold back in saying some honest things about each child—all in poetic form. (Notice the text of your Bible here. In most Bibles you will see this set in stanzas as poetry, rather than in blocks of prose text.)

Look at verses 9–10, where Israel talks about Judah. (And remember how Judah's progeny happened, through Tamar, who had to pose as a prostitute to bring about the next generation.) "Judah, my son, is a young lion that has finished eating its prey. Like a lion he crouches and lies down; like a lioness—who dares to rouse him? The scepter will not depart from Judah, nor the ruler's staff from his descendants, until the coming of the one to whom it belongs, the one whom all nations will honor." This is a foreshadowing of the lineage of Jesus Christ. We see Israel's prophetic utterance fulfilled in Matthew 1:3, in the passage delineating the ancestors of Jesus: "Judah was the father of Perez and Zerah (whose mother was Tamar)."

Like Joseph's other brothers, Judah was deeply flawed, and yet God uses his progeny as a precursor to the savior of the world. What hope that conveys to all of us. No matter what we do, we cannot thwart the plans of the Almighty God. His will persists, despite our frailty and propensity to sin.

We see the blessing of Joseph in Genesis 49:22–26, where Israel retells his story. He says of Joseph, "But his bow remained taut, and his arms were strengthened" (v. 24). His brothers harmed him, maligned him, wronged him, but he remained resolute. We see the culmination of this blessing when Joseph utters those famous words in Genesis 50:20, "You intended to harm me, but God intended it all for good." His is a mark of spiritual maturity—an encouragement to us as we look back on our own journeys and trace the hand of God's faithfulness through them.

Truth: People may have intended to harm you. Truth: Walking through betrayal deeply affected you. Even bigger truth: God used that trial to grow you, mature you, and empower you to forgive and bring help to others.

Lord, help me remember today that my regrets don't prevent your regeneration. I cannot ruin your plan. Thank you for choosing me, frail as I am, to help others. I pray you would grow me up like Joseph so that when trials come (and they will!), my bow will remain taut, and my arms (and heart) will be strengthened. I want to persevere well. Amen.

GOD DOES THE MIRACULOUS

○ **Morning:** Exodus 1–6
○ **Noon:** Exodus 7–12
○ **Night:** Psalm 7

Today we meet Moses, whose name means the drawing out of or pulling out of water. In Samuel Taylor Coleridge's famous poem "The Rime of the Ancient Mariner," he writes, "Water, water, everywhere, / Nor any drop to drink." If you look at today's reading through the lens of water, blurry as that might be, you'll see some fascinating coincidences.

First, Moses is placed in the waters of the Nile when Pharaoh orders the killing of Israelite children. Remember, this is the same kind of ordered infanticide we find Jesus subject to after he is born.

Moses is rescued from the water by the daughter of the one who wanted him killed.

After he grows up, Moses kills an Egyptian in an attempt to be a deliverer before his time; he flees to Midian and sits beside a water source (a well), where he helps the daughters of a priest. They tell their father, Reuel, "An Egyptian rescued us from the shepherds," adding, "And then he drew water for us and watered our flocks" (Exodus 2:19).

Later, when Moses returns to Egypt, many of his miracles involve the waters of the Nile, the very body of water from which he was rescued. Of course, tomorrow we'll read about the great deliverance of the Israelites through the Red Sea.

Why is water so important in the life of Moses? And what does it mean for us? As I mentioned in the introduction, my husband reminds me that you can't read the book of Romans without knowing the story of the exodus, pre–Red Sea, mid–Red Sea, and post–Red Sea.

Water is the substance of life. Without it, we will die. But it also is highly symbolic in the life of a believer, particularly as we look at the life of Jesus. While Moses was a Levite (a priest) by blood, Jesus was the Great High Priest who turned water into wine.

Jesus submitted to the waters of baptism. He triumphed over the laws of physics by walking upon water. He told his disciples he is the Living Water (see John 7:37–38; John 4). He reminded his followers, "And if you give even a cup of cold water to one of the least of my followers, you will surely be rewarded" (Matthew 10:42). And after he died, water and blood poured from his side (see John 19:34).

As you read through the Bible in this brisk plan, take note of water. See how it splashes onto the pages of Scripture. And don't forget to run to the source of Living Water, Jesus himself, who fills every nook and cranny of our needs, satiating us with that which truly satisfies. As you will read in John 7:37–39, he told the crowds at a festival, "Anyone who is thirsty may come to me! Anyone who believes in me may come and drink! For the Scriptures declare, 'Rivers of living water will flow from his heart.' (When he said, 'living water,' he was speaking for the Spirit, who would be given to everyone believing in him.)"

The very Holy Spirit of God will be the One empowering you to continue this Bible reading challenge, satisfying your longings, and bringing you life.

> *Lord, help me to marvel at the synchronicity of your Word. Open my eyes to connections, metaphors, and themes that repeat throughout Scripture. Thank you for truly, deeply satisfying the longings of my soul. Amen.*

GOD GENTLY LEADS HIS PEOPLE

○ **Morning:** Exodus 13–19
○ **Noon:** Exodus 20–24
○ **Night:** Psalms 8–9

God is a gentle leader; he knows what we need. He is aware of our fears and worries. In today's passage we see different aspects of his kindhearted character with the nation of Israel. Because he is omnipresent (everywhere) and omniscient (all knowing) and omnipotent (all powerful), he knows best how to lead his people through perils.

God leads through logic. In Exodus 13:17–18, we see that God doesn't lead the Israelites through the Philistine territory because a battle right away would cause them to turn and run back to Egypt. "So God led them in a roundabout way through the wilderness toward the Red Sea" (v. 18). The parallels to our own lives are numerous. Have you ever wondered why you were in an oxymoronic place, where nothing made sense, only to realize later the meaning of the roundabout path God led you through?

God woos through signs. In Exodus 13:21–23, we read that God blazes the trail before the wandering Israelites in a cloud pillar by day and a fire pillar by night. No matter where they were, they could see the Lord ahead of them. God goes before you too. He knows the path you will take. And he loves to guide you.

God leads with power. In Exodus 14, we see a grand deliverance, the God of the universe walling up the waters of the Red Sea so the nation could pass through it on dry ground, then covering over their enemies with a rush of water. Likewise, God did what we could not do by sending his son, Jesus, to die for us, making a pathway where none existed.

God guides because of his kindness. Moses sings, "With your unfailing love you lead the people you have redeemed. In your might, you guide them to your sacred home" (Exodus 15:13). God leads his people (including you) with love and compassion.

God also leads through provision. In Exodus 16, he provides bread (manna) and meat (quail) to the complaining Israelites. In chapter 17, God provides life-giving water to the nation. They could not continue their journey without it. Jesus is both our bread and water of life, the wellspring of our souls. His provision gives us the strength we need to follow him into difficult places. He declared, "I am the bread of life. Whoever comes to me will never be hungry again. Whoever believes in me will never be thirsty" (John 6:35).

God leads through instruction in the Decalogue (Ten Commandments) in Exodus 20:2–17. In order for the Israelites to know how to be and what to do, God clearly shares his commands with a nation prone to wander. In Jesus Christ, he beautifully fulfills the Law and the Prophets, satisfying the sacrificial system so that we can instinctively (with the Spirit within us) follow him on new journeys.

Lord, thank you for the different ways you lead your people. I am grateful you're so gentle when you lead me. I pray you would provide for me and my family. I pray you would help me see you amid my difficult journey. I trust you to show me the next step. Amen.

GOD LOVES TO DWELL WITH US

○ **Morning:** Exodus 25–29
○ **Noon:** Exodus 30–34
○ **Night:** Psalm 10

Isn't it amazing that God wants to dwell with us? He loves to be near, and he helps us find him in a variety of ways. Even though sin reigned in the world from the moment Adam and Eve tasted the forbidden fruit, severing fellowship with their Creator, God still pursued them and wanted to be involved in their lives.

While the nation of Israel moved from place to place, following God's presence in the form of a cloud or fire, we now see how God wants to interact with the nation through a special tent. The tabernacle represents the moveable and nimble presence of God. Wherever Israel ventures, they can find God in each new place. Later, when the nation settles into the Promised Land, that movable tent will become a temple under the skillful hands of its second king, Solomon.

Because God is holy, humankind could not just jump into his presence. There needed to be a sacred place for his presence to dwell, with intermediaries (priests) acting as liaisons between a holy God and an unholy people.

The various elements of the tabernacle (which will be echoed in the temple) reveal what we must walk through to enter the presence of a holy God. The altar is the place where sacrifice for sin is displayed and practiced. The washbasin reminds us that we are unclean and in need of washing. The lampstand echoes the importance of walking in the light (remembering that sin is darkness). The table inside the Holy Place reveals our dependency on God for daily sustenance (bread). The incense altar represents our prayers dependent upon the Lord. The curtain drawn between the Holy Place and the Most Holy Place shows us that there is a true distinction between our unholy selves and our holy God. We cannot just rend it and walk in. The ark of the covenant reminds the Israelites that they are a covenantal people, with God as their King.

Today, Jesus is our intermediary. He has sacrificed himself on the altar of the cross. Through his blood, we are washed clean. When he walked the earth, Jesus not only fed thousands of people, but he called himself the Bread of Life, the sustainer of our hearts. Post-resurrection, he now prays for us at the right hand of the Father (he prays for us!), and he gives us the Holy Spirit who also intercedes for us. At the moment of his death, the veil of the temple between the Holy Place and the Most Holy Place was torn in two, allowing unfettered access into the New Covenant, where we are welcomed, loved, forgiven, and communed with.

Isn't it beautiful how the Old Testament is a shadow of what will come?

Lord, thank you for showing me the different parts of the tabernacle. Remind me of the privilege it is that I can have unfettered access to you. Thank you for interceding for me. Help me live my life in light of the beautiful New Covenant you inaugurated through your life, death, and resurrection. Amen.

GOD LOVES OUR OFFERINGS

○ **Morning:** Exodus 35–40
○ **Noon:** Leviticus 1–10
○ **Night:** Psalm 11

We are meant to live in community, and in that community, to worship and serve the One who created us. But what does that look like? And what can we learn from the various offerings we read about today?

In this section, we read about several ways the nation of Israel could show their devotion to God: the burnt offering, grain offering, peace offering, sin offering, and guilt offering.

In the burnt offering, the priest presents a perfect bull, ram, or male bird to restore a worshiper with their God. The death of that sacrifice reinstates a person with their community. We see the purpose of this offering detailed in Leviticus 4:20, "Through this process, the priest will purify the people, making them right with the LORD, and they will be forgiven."

The grain offering does not take away sin or restore worship. It is a demonstration of gratitude for the provision God offers. Israelites were to bring flour (or bread), olive oil, frankincense, and salt as a thank-you to God. It reveals the person's dependence on God for everything. It is an act of worship. (Notice how worship weaves its way through these sacrifices?)

The peace offering represents the kind of fellowship we are to have with others. This is an offering of meat and bread in order to share a meal with others in the community. This, too, is an act of worship, thanking God for both provision and relationships.[1]

The sin offering is an atoning sacrifice (with a goal similar to that of the burnt offering). To atone means to reconcile or restore the relationship between a holy God and a sinful person. The animal acts as an intermediary between the two parties. This offering covered unintentional sins as well.

The guilt offering, also an atoning offering, uses a perfect lamb or ram to pay for sins committed both against God and against other people in the community. This offering atones for both.

The goal of the sacrificial system was to create *shalom*, a Hebrew word that means wholeness and restoration. The tabernacle and its sacrifices were a shadow of what would eventually happen when a Greater One would become all these offerings on behalf of a sinful humanity. Hebrews 9:23–24 reminds us, "That is why the Tabernacle and everything in it, which were copies of things in heaven, had to be purified by the blood of animals. But the real things in heaven had to be purified with far better sacrifices than the blood of animals. For Christ did not enter into a holy place made with human hands, which was only a copy of the true one in heaven. He entered into heaven itself to appear now before God on our behalf."

Lord, I'm so grateful for restoration. I can't thank you enough for being the culmination of the entire sacrificial system all by yourself, offering me freedom from sin and fellowship with others. You did it all. I know I could not atone for myself, but you, in your kindness, atoned for me and the whole world. I stand amazed. I love you, and I worship you. Amen.

Day 9

GOD CLEANSES US

○ **Morning:** Leviticus 11–16
○ **Noon:** Leviticus 17–20
○ **Night:** Psalms 12–13

God is completely *other* than us. That's what holiness means. He is clean; we are not. He is sovereign; we are not. He is all-powerful; we are not. *Other.*

In today's reading we learn a lot about what is clean and what is unclean. Another way to look at cleanness is to think of orderliness. What is clean (holy) is what is normal, orderly, or how it should be. What is unclean is abnormal, disorderly, or represents how things should *not* be. God created these seemingly random laws because he is a God of order. And he wanted the nation of Israel to be utterly distinct—to be holy as he is holy, to be a bastion of order.

Reading this passage with Acts 10 in mind will help you work through the intent of these cleanliness and food laws. There we see Peter, a devout Jew who has never eaten anything unclean, being faced with a sheet coming from heaven filled with all the animals prohibited in the Levitical laws. God tells him, "Get up, Peter; kill and eat them" (v. 13).

Scripture tells us that "Peter was very perplexed" (v. 17). He experiences this sheet/animal vision three times, yet all three times, God commands him to do something Peter considers unclean. God tells him, "Do not call something unclean if God has made it clean" (v. 15).

The story ends with Peter having a meeting with a Gentile (someone perceived as unclean) and the church spreading beyond the nation of Israel to the rest of the world. It had been God's intention all along that Israel would be a city on a hill, beckoning lost humanity to the God who created them. But Israel did not fulfill this ministry. And it wasn't until after the life, death, and resurrection of Jesus that we see the true fulfillment of this amazing purpose. That which was unholy (whether Jew or Gentile) was made holy through Jesus Christ, inaugurating a brand-new community, the church.

God remains an orderly God. In 1 Corinthians 14:33, 40, Paul writes, "For God is not a God of disorder but of peace, as in all the meetings of God's holy people. . . . But be sure that everything is done properly and in order."

When we see the commencement of the church, perhaps that's why we encounter such judgment when Ananias and Sapphira lie about the money they held back in Acts chapter 5. God's holiness did not change from the Old to the New Testament. The result of the deaths of Ananias and Sapphira ushered in a holy hush. "Great fear gripped the entire church and everyone else who heard what had happened" (Acts 5:11).

While we are free from the Levitical dietary laws in this new era of grace, we still serve and worship a God of order and holiness. We must remember he is *other* than us and revere him accordingly.

> Lord, thank you that you are a God of order. I am grateful you are other than me. In light of that, search my heart, help me to see you for who you are, and empower me to love you well. I'm grateful you hold the whole world in the palm of your capable hand. I can trust you. Thank you for setting me free from dietary restrictions, but even more, thank you for simply setting me free from the tyranny of sin. Amen.

GOD LOVES CELEBRATIONS

○ **Morning:** Leviticus 21–27
○ **Noon:** Numbers 1–4
○ **Night:** Psalms 14–15

In our world, we've lost the art of celebration. Not all denominations operate from a church calendar, with rhythms of rejoicing, remembering, and recognizing. Considering that, it's wholly instructive to look at the yearly festivals outlined in the Torah (the first five books of the Bible).

Perhaps the most famous annual festival is the Passover remembrance. It occurred during March or April of the calendar year as a celebration of God's deliverance of the Israelites from Egypt. The last trial Moses enacted (through the Lord) on the Egyptians was the death of its firstborn. Only those with lamb's blood painted over the doorposts of a home escaped the death angel. They celebrated this deliverance by refraining from eating anything with yeast and sacrificing a Passover lamb, among other practices. When we celebrate the Lord's Supper, we mimic many of the elements of the Passover seder, revealing how Jesus truly was our Passover Lamb who delivered us from death to life.

There are three harvest festivals throughout the Jewish calendar: First Fruits, Pentecost, and Shelters (Booths). As the first one demonstrates in its name, it's a festival during which people offer the very best and first of their harvest. It's a sign of trust that God is their provider. We see powerful fulfillment of this when Jesus feeds many people and calls himself the Bread of Life. The Pentecost festival, also known as the festival of weeks or the festival of the harvest, comes fifty days after First Fruits at the end of the grain harvest. This is when the Israelites renew their covenant with God as they honor him with the abundance of their crop. Interestingly, the church started on the Day of Pentecost when a New Covenant was truly lived out. The Booths festival signifies the final harvest of the year. Living for seven days "outside in little shelters" (Leviticus 23:42) was a reminder to Israel that they once wandered in the wilderness. What's instructive is to read all the gospels with these festivals in mind. You'll see them peppered throughout the narrative. How beautiful that Jesus celebrated them all!

The Festival of Trumpets (Rosh Hashanah) is celebrated in September or October with loud trumpet blasts (hence the name) and a holy assembly on a special Sabbath day, reminding the Israelites that God works on their behalf. The Day of Atonement (Yom Kippur) is the year's most important festival when people fast on the Sabbath and the high priest makes atonement for all of Israel's sins.

Read simply with Jesus in mind, we see how beautifully Jesus fulfills these festivals, both by participating in them as a good Jew and by embodying them. He is our Deliverer, whose blood was shed on our behalf. He feeds us, provides for us, shelters us, and atones for us. What a beautiful Savior!

> *Lord, I want to have a rhythm in my life, to celebrate you and all you've done throughout the year. Thank you for being the fulfillment of these festivals—for shedding your blood for me, for providing for my family, and for experiencing so much strife on my behalf. I'm humbled and awed by all you've done for me. Amen.*

GOD DESIRES TO BLESS US

○ **Morning:** Numbers 5–10
○ **Noon:** Numbers 11–16
○ **Night:** Psalms 16–17

One of the most famous passages of the Bible is found in today's reading. The Lord compelled Moses to ask Aaron and his sons to proclaim these words over the nation of Israel: "May the LORD bless you and protect you. May the LORD smile on you and be gracious to you. May the LORD show you his favor and give you his peace" (Numbers 6:24–26). The Lord adds, "Whenever Aaron and his sons bless the people of Israel in my name, I myself will bless them" (v. 27).

We see this blessing *prior to* the nation of Israel's testing, and that pattern often happens in our own lives as well—blessing, then testing. The Israelites are on the move, stepping into new territory. They may be frightened or hold a strong fear of the unknown. Can you relate? Are you in a place of doing something brand new, where God has beckoned you to a new level of trust? That's the situation the nation of Israel faced, so prior to that, the Lord, in his kindhearted wisdom, showered blessing upon them.

Unfortunately for the Israelites (and for us), when we're faced with new battles, we tend to resort to fear. And fear, when it takes root, causes us to grumble and complain. In Numbers 11 and 12, we see complaint in its full vent. "Soon the people began to complain about their hardship, and the Lord heard everything they said" (Numbers 11:1). They worried about provision, having forgotten the proclaimed blessing of provision and favor. God granted them food, but then Miriam and Aaron joined in the complaint, this time leveling criticism at Moses. (God ended up defending Moses and chastising his sister and brother.)

The blessing they'd received at the onset of their journey became as silent as a whisper on the wind. The fear they gave in to fanned into rebellion in Numbers 14 and 16. It wasn't long before the Israelites pined for the "good old days" in Egypt, completely forgetting the mighty deliverance God had given them.

This is a pattern for us as well. We are deeply, profoundly blessed by the God who created us. We forget the truth of that blessing, which then leads to fear. Fear causes complaint and forgetfulness. When we stop remembering God's goodness and provision, when the blessing is merely an echo of the past, we are prone to rebel, to outwardly walk away from the path God has created for us.

This is why you see throughout the Bible the ongoing command to remember. To not give in to selective forgetfulness. To go back and recount the ways God has delivered us from peril and mayhem. He is able. We must remember his abilities to deliver us. Perhaps part of that remembering is reciting this beautiful blessing every day over yourself and your family. God is for you. He loves to protect you, smile upon you, and shower you with graciousness. He longs to give you peace and favor. Rest there.

Lord, may today's reading remind me to remember your blessing. To not forget all you have done for me. Forgive me for giving in to fear, for forgetting your many deliverances. Lord, I want to remember. I want to be faithful to you because you've been so faithful to me. Amen.

⊘ Day 12

GOD USES UN-FOLLOWERS

- ○ **Morning:** Numbers 17–21
- ○ **Noon:** Numbers 22–27
- ○ **Night:** Psalm 18

We see the story of Balaam in today's reading. He is known as a diviner, someone who reads signs and who conjures up the future as a seer. The king of Moab, Balak, hired Balaam to curse Israel. That didn't go over so well. Because even a diviner is under the power and might of God, Balaam could not help but reverse that curse and utter a blessing instead. "God is not a man, so he does not lie. He is not human, so he does not change his mind. Has he ever spoken and failed to act? Has he ever promised and not carried it through? Listen, I received a command to bless; God has blessed, and I cannot reverse it!" (Numbers 23:19–20).

Balaam is also known for being rebuked by a talking donkey. Here we see that even someone who is not following the Lord (and is, in fact, actively opposing him) cannot obscure the presence of God. God's plans can never be thwarted by mere human activity.

It's instructive to learn more about Balaam throughout the Bible. In Nehemiah 13:2, the wall-builder refers to the Moabites when he writes, "For they had not provided the Israelites with food and water in the wilderness. Instead, they hired Balaam to curse them, though our God turned the curse into a blessing."

Later, in 2 Peter 2:15–16, we learn this about Balaam: "They have wandered off the right road and followed the footsteps of Balaam son of Beor, who loved to earn money by doing wrong. But Balaam was stopped from his mad course when his donkey rebuked him with a human voice."

Tucked into the middle of Jude 1:11, we read, "Like Balaam, they deceive people for money." And in Revelation 2:14, we see the pervasive evil of Balaam when John speaks to Pergamum, a church prone to compromise. "But I have a few complaints against you. You tolerate some among you whose teaching is like that of Balaam, who showed Balak how to trip up the people of Israel. He taught them to sin by eating food offered to idols and by committing sexual sin."

The beautiful truth of these frustrating pictures of Balaam is this: God will prevail, even when human beings do their best to bring about their own will. God can use opposing kings, rebellious diviners, and even unsuspecting donkeys to bring about deliverance and help. As in the story of the Israelites who eventually gave in to sin, we also see the seductive power of it. We should heed this and be on the alert. If we zoom out, however, we see that God even used the exile in the life of Israel to bring about deliverance. It was through that nation that the Savior of the world was born.

Even evil intent cannot undermine the plan of God!

Lord, I give you the people in my life who have acted like Balaam—absorbed in money, prone to sin, and eager to incite rebellion. Please keep me close to you so I can honor you with my life. I am grateful you have a plan that you can even use the evil others do to bring about something beautiful. Help me be patient as I wait for that resolution. Amen.

✓ Day 13

GOD RECEIVES OUR OFFERINGS

○ **Morning:** Numbers 28–31
○ **Noon:** Numbers 32–36
○ **Night:** Psalms 19–20

Throughout Numbers we see a wide variety of offerings the Israelites gave to their God. Daily they were to present what Moses calls "special gifts" that are a "pleasing aroma" to God (see Numbers 28:1–2). These daily gifts involved livestock, grain, and drink—the elements of a meal and a symbol of trust.

Could it be that these offerings represented a community meal between God and humanity? There is nothing more satisfying when you're famished than sitting down to a spread of food in the company of others. Imagine supping with the God of the universe!

These daily offerings telescoped toward Jesus's meals with his disciples—some that he provided miraculously, others that came through the hands of others.

And it echoes forward toward the marriage supper of the Lamb in Revelation 19. "Praise the LORD! For the Lord our God, the Almighty, reigns. Let us be glad and rejoice, and let us give honor to him. For the time has come for the wedding feast of the Lamb, and his bride has prepared herself" (Revelation 19:6–7). Someday there will be a feast we eat when we are perfectly complete and whole! Imagine how that will be—no dividing line between us and the Lord. We will be his bride, invited to the best banquet ever experienced on earth.

These daily offerings are also a symbol of Israel's trust in God as provider. When you let go of wealth (in this case with livestock, grain, and drink), you reveal that you're not trusting in riches to provide for you. Your relinquishment reveals your trust.

But these symbols of trust also involve sacrifice. It's not merely that you're demonstrating trust in God's provision, but you're revealing that you're willing to give your very best to the Lord— because you love him and want to worship him.

God built into the calendar of the Israelites consistent opportunities to worship him this way—daily, weekly on the Sabbath, monthly, yearly, and throughout the various stages of the harvest. This was a rhythm of offerings, a pattern of giving and trust that served them well as they entered the Promised Land.

We have these kinds of rhythms today when we offer the first fruits of our modern-day harvests (tithes and offerings). We do this to show we realize God is our provider and to reveal the worshipful nature of our hearts. We offer ourselves to God through prayer and surrender. We sing praises to God as we go about our days, and we eat meals with others in celebration of all he has done for us. We do this in anticipation of the coming kingdom, while we seek to see God do on earth what he is already doing in heaven.

Lord, I want to have a rhythm of offering. Help me remember to give you the very best of what I have. Prompt me to invite others over for a meal. Thank you that Jesus also experienced these same offerings, but also offered himself for his people. He provided a banquet of forgiveness for us all, and for that, I am grateful. Amen.

Day 14

GOD WANTS US TO REMEMBER AND OBEY

○ **Morning:** Deuteronomy 1–6
○ **Noon:** Deuteronomy 7–12
○ **Night:** Psalm 21

These beginning chapters of Deuteronomy are Moses's recounting of God's extreme faithfulness to the nation of Israel. Throughout the Old and New Testaments, we are reminded to remember. God knows that to remember his goodness and provision helps keep us from straying. You can almost hear Moses's heartbeat and longing in these chapters. Remembering helps us obey. Forgetting leads to fretting, then to disobedience.

Chapter 8 is a pivotal chapter that details God's faithfulness. "Remember how the Lord your God led you through the wilderness for these forty years, humbling you and testing you to prove your character, and to find out whether or not you would obey his commands" (v. 2). When you walk through a difficult time, it's important to remember that God has other motives beneath what you see on the surface. He is testing you, helping you see what you're made of. This crucible of character gives you strength to face the next battles ahead.

Moses reminded the Israelites that God was their provider, the one who gave manna to them in the wilderness. The Hebrew word for manna simply means "What is it?"[1] God provided supernaturally in a surprising, winsome way. When Jesus was tempted by the devil in the wilderness, he quoted from Deuteronomy 8:3, "He did it to teach you that people do not live by bread alone; rather, we live by every word that comes from the mouth of the Lord."

Again, you see how all the lessons of wandering were meant to prepare the people of God to obey.

God also provided for the Israelites in the form of the kind of footwear that miraculously did not wear out. Not only that, but those who wore the sandals did not get blisters. This act of provision moved beyond the physical act of giving non-decaying shoes, protecting the health of the Israelites; open sores on feet spelled trouble, even doom.

In light of remembering, what else does God require of his people? In 8:10–14, Moses reminds them that they are to praise God for all he has done. "For when you have become full and prosperous and have built fine homes to live in, and when your flocks and herds have become very large and your silver and gold have multiplied along with everything else, be careful! Do not become proud at that time and forget the Lord your God, who rescued you from slavery in the land of Egypt" (8:12–14). To remember and praise is to prevent a proud, self-absorbed heart. Everything we have is a gift from God. To live as if we have created that wealth is to forget the beautiful provision of God. He warns, "He did all this so you would never say to yourself, 'I have achieved this wealth with my own strength and energy'" (8:17).

These lessons are repeated throughout Scripture. Remember. Recount. Think on. Praise God. Don't forget. May today be a day of remembrance that fuels obedience.

> *Lord, thank you for showing me the pattern of obedience, that I am to remember physical and food provision and the way you have led me thus far, and that I am to praise you for every way you have helped me. I don't want to become proud, forgetting all that you've done. I love you and I'm grateful for you. Amen.*

✓ Day 15

GOD PROVIDES REFUGE

◯ **Morning:** Deuteronomy 13–18
◯ **Noon:** Deuteronomy 19–23
◯ **Night:** Psalm 22

In this passage, we learn more about the concept (and reality) of cities of refuge. Interestingly, there were supposed to be more cities added by the nation of Israel, but they only managed to create six. All six were manned by the Levitical priests. Those cities were Golan, Ramoth, Bezer, Kedesh, Shechem, and Hebron. These places surrounded the sea of Galilee, the Jordan, and the Dead Sea.

In these cities of refuge, people who did not premeditate a murder could flee for refuge until the court system could enact a just response. Apparently, the roads leading to each city were to be beautifully maintained, so it would not be difficult for a fugitive to flee to them.

These cities were created because of the *Lex Talionis,* or the Law of Retaliation cited in Exodus 21 and Leviticus 24. Basically, if someone poked out an eye, the other person's eye would be poked out as an act of justice. If someone killed another person, the person responsible for the murder was to be killed. Like punishment for like crime.

However, there were instances when a person randomly killed someone by accident, with no ill intent, no malice, no premeditation. In that case, they could flee to a city of refuge, where they were promised fair treatment.

Considering all that, it's interesting to think of Jesus as our city of refuge. We are captive to sin, deserving justice, and yet Jesus offers himself as that safe place to run to when we've come to the end of ourselves, know our need for a savior, and cannot pay the penalty for the mountain of sin against a holy God.

Many times throughout the Psalms, we read of this sheltering aspect of the Lord. "God is our refuge and strength, always ready to help in times of trouble" (Psalm 46:1). Later, in Psalm 91, we learn we can actually make God our shelter. "If you make the LORD your refuge, if you make the Most High your shelter, no evil will conquer you; no plague will come near your home" (vv. 9–10).

How amazing that God created physical places on earth where people could run for protection, all along embodying that protection in his character. This is the God we serve, a God who provides refuge and help when we need it.

> *Lord, thank you for providing a way for those who didn't intend to harm someone. Thank you for providing justice and mercy in your cities of refuge. I choose today to see you as my refuge, from the conspiracies of words, from the difficulties of stress, and from my own penchant to choose sin rather than you. Please be my refuge today. Amen.*

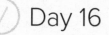 Day 16

GOD LOVES THE QUARTET OF THE VULNERABLE

Morning: Deuteronomy 24–28
Noon: Deuteronomy 29–34
Night: Psalms 23–24

God intended the nation of Israel to be a city on a hill, a place and community that displayed his winsome heart. God's heart has always been to woo an errant humanity to himself. In the Old Testament, he operated through the community of Israel. In the New Testament, he revealed his compassion through the church.

If you read the entire Bible through the lens of what scholars call *the quartet of the vulnerable*, you'll see the kindness of God on display. This quartet is the poor, the widow, the orphan, and the alien. These are people who cannot help themselves, and God has tasked his people to care for them. This reveals the kind of God he is—one of compassion and care.

This care for the quartet also has an element of remembrance in it. The Israelites were enslaved with no agency in Egypt. They had no help for many years. God gloriously set them free, then tasked them to be utterly different from the enslavers. Whereas the Egyptians stripped Israel of its agency, the Israelites were to prefer those who had no agency.

In any society, there are haves and have-nots. And so many times, the haves oppress the have-nots. But often throughout Scripture, God warns his people not to allow bribes from the rich or to pervert the ways of justice to favor the powerful.

God's ethic for us all is to have scruples, to not create differing weights of measure for different people, to care for those who cannot feed themselves, to elevate the rights of those seemingly without rights.

The prophets often brought this idea of kindness and compassion back to the Israelites, saying things like: "Learn to do good. Seek justice. Help the oppressed. Defend the cause of orphans. Fight for the rights of widows" (Isaiah 1:17). They were especially blunt when Israel couched their lack of concern under religious activities. "At their religious festivals, they lounge in clothing their debtors put up as security. In the house of their gods, they drink wine bought with unjust fines" (Amos 2:8).

Later we see Jesus bring up these injustices to the Pharisees, saying, "What sorrow awaits you teachers of religious law and you Pharisees. Hypocrites! For you are careful to tithe even the tiniest income from your herb gardens, but you ignore the more important aspects of the law—justice, mercy, and faith. You should tithe, yes, but do not neglect the more important things" (Matthew 23:23).

These "more important aspects" are the heartbeat of God. To neglect the orphan, widow, poor, and alien is to reject the God who made them. We are called to be the hand of God in a disgracefully unjust world. And even today, we are demonstrating the love of God when we care for those who cannot care for themselves.

Lord, help me remember the quartet of the vulnerable when I read through your Word. It's a lens I know is necessary because it reveals your heart. Please awaken me to the broken in my own community. And I pray for tangible ways to love the people in my world. Amen.

GOD KEEPS HIS PROMISES

○ **Morning:** Joshua 1–10
○ **Noon:** Joshua 11–21
○ **Night:** Psalm 25

In today's reading we see the beginning of the conquest of Canaan, inaugurating with a dramatic capturing of Jericho. But there is a beautiful gem in this story that should encourage you. It's the story of Rahab, known as a prostitute. Though she was certainly not an Israelite, she had heard of the exploits of the Lord. So she demonstrated an unusual faith in the God who provided such deliverance.

In every way, she feared God.

She protected the spies.

She spoke of God's power and greatness.

She had confidence in God's ability to deliver the town of Jericho into the hands of the Israelites.

She demonstrated God's *hesed*, his loyal love, as she asked the spies to promise to protect her family.

She put herself in danger to take care of her guests—in that way, she practiced unusual hospitality.

She asked the spies to swear on God's name that they would be just.

She hoisted the men down the wall to send them another way. She did this to preserve them as well as the nation they represented.

She feared God more than she feared her king.

All this occurs in Joshua chapter 2. Later, in Joshua chapter 6, we see Joshua embodying an emissary of God's promise: "Keep your promise. Go to the prostitute's house and bring her out, along with her family" (Joshua 6:22).

Here we see the covenantal nature of God, his loyal love even to those outside the commonwealth of Israel. What's beautiful is that Rahab marries into the nation (some believe she married one of the spies), then gives birth to Boaz, the grandfather of King David's father, Jesse. Though Rahab was an outsider, God brought her into the fold. He kept his promise. Not only that, but Rahab is also part of the lineage of Jesus Christ.

Isn't it amazing that God does not punish or banish outsiders? He is seeking people who believe him, who revere him, who dare to follow him even when it costs them something. Our God keeps his promises, and he loves to lead his people toward life and hope.

Rahab is a necessary reminder that God's heart for the world he created is not narrowed to one nation. He seeks faithful followers everywhere. "The eyes of the LORD search the whole earth in order to strengthen those whose hearts are fully committed to him" (2 Chronicles 16:9). No matter what your station in life, no matter what other people say about you, God is most interested in your heart toward him and your belief in his promises.

Lord, thank you for listening to, protecting, and empowering Rahab—an outsider. She gives me hope that you are far more interested in the hearts of people than their station in life. I pray you would strengthen my heart—a heart I hope is fully committed to you. Help me as I rapid-read your Word to really understand the power of a promise kept. Amen.

✓ Day 18

GOD CHOOSES DIFFERENTLY

○ **Morning:** Joshua 22–24
○ **Noon:** Judges 1–8
○ **Night:** Psalm 26

As of today, you've successfully read 20 percent of the Bible. What an accomplishment! You may be surprised to know that three of the Bible's most unlikely heroes decorate the pages of your reading: Deborah, Jael, and Gideon.

Deborah holds two distinctions—as a prophet of God and a judge of her nation. In other words, she's heavenly minded *and* practices earthly good. In a patriarchal society that placed far more emphasis and favor upon the men in a tribe, God's choosing of Deborah borders on shocking. She is seen as a woman of valor, one who brings strategic victory to her people, even as Barak shrinks from his military duties. Her song in Judges 5 reflects her fidelity to the Lord and her ability to endure difficult circumstances. She writes, "March on with courage, my soul" (v. 21) and "But may those who love you rise like the sun in all its power" (v. 31). She demonstrates an uncanny obedience to God and a fearless demeanor in encountering Israel's enemies.

Jael, too, is an unlikely person to carry out the justice of God. The wife of someone empathetic to Sisera (Israel's enemy), she invites the king into her home, supposedly as a safe haven. Deborah writes of Jael's impaling of Sisera with a tent peg when she sings, "Sisera asked for water, and she gave him milk. In a bowl fit for nobles, she brought him yogurt. Then with her left hand she reached for a tent peg, and with her right hand for the workman's hammer. She struck Sisera with the hammer, crushing his head. With a shattering blow, she pierced his temples" (Judges 5:25–26).

Later, we're introduced to Gideon, hiding in a winepress, secretly threshing wheat because the Midianites were systematically starving the Israelites. An angel of the Lord prophecies, telling Gideon, "Mighty hero, the LORD is with you" (Judges 6:12). Though he is the weakest member of the smallest, most insignificant tribe, God chooses him to not only tear down altars to idols, but to also free Israel from the clutches of Midian. How beautiful that God selects the least likely to do his best work! And just in case Gideon had opportunity to boast of his exploits, the Lord whittles down his army from 32,000 to 300, revealing this truth: God is bigger than humankind. He is larger than the largest, scariest army. He is more powerful than the greatest weapons.

In the case of Deborah and Jael, we read, "Then there was peace in the land for forty years" (Judges 5:31). In Gideon's life, we see him starting with fear (hiding), to practicing great faithfulness (tearing down the altars), then achieving a wartime victory. But he does not finish well. He worships an ephod he creates, reminding us just how easy it is to slip into Paul's warnings. "So they worshiped and served the things God created instead of the Creator himself, who is worthy of eternal praise! Amen" (Romans 1:25).

We must remember, in this journey of brisk Bible reading, that often the Bible is descriptive—showing us cautionary tales of those who strayed. In cases like those, we can learn what *not* to do as we follow after Jesus.

Lord, thank you for choosing unlikely people to carry out your plans. That gives me hope that perhaps you can use me too in my context to bring light to dark places. Help me be faithful like Deborah, Jael, and Gideon, but also empower me to finish well, unlike Gideon. Amen.

✓ Day 19

GOD RESCUES THE REPENTANT

○ **Morning:** Judges 9–16
○ **Noon:** Judges 17–21
○ **Night:** Psalm 27

You've made great progress through the book of Judges. Congratulations! As you read it, you may have uncovered a frustrating pattern, what scholars call *the cycle of the judges*. The nation of Israel, prone to apostasy, usually starts off well, with great intention to obey God and follow him all the days of their lives. The book begins with a war, when, after the death of their leader Joshua, they inquire of God what to do next, who to invade. God answers their inquiry; they obey—but not fully. This penchant for partial obedience inaugurates the cycle.

Here's what the cycle looks like. The nation of Israel starts with obedience, then shifts toward disobedience. Because of that straying, God disciplines the nation, usually through oppression by their enemies. The Israelites cry out in pain and distress, asking God to please deliver them. Our compassionate God chooses to deliver them, usually by lifting up a new judge who will lead them well and free them from oppression. Rejoicing follows, celebrating the kindness of God. All is well until disobedience (sadly) comes roaring back, and the cycle continues. Obedience. Disobedience. Discipline. Crying out. Deliverance. Praise. Repeat.

This reading may remind you of the times before Noah, when people did whatever they wanted. In this instance, God hems them in with judges, but no matter how powerful or godly the deliverer, they cannot sustain righteousness for an entire nation.

This impossibility of one person creating righteousness for many points us forward—to realizing Jesus did just that. He interrupted the cycle of the judges at the point of our disobedience. He exemplified perfect obedience. He then took the discipline of his Father, who must punish sin. On the cross, our perfect Jesus cried out for deliverance, yet he suffered death once and for all. The result? Praise from us, his people whom he has made righteous and whole.

The book of Judges ends on an ominous note. "In those days Israel had no king; all the people did whatever seemed right in their own eyes" (Judges 21:25). It's the setup for what will come next—a king. You can almost hear the hope in that despairing statement, that perhaps a king would change everything. Perhaps then Israel would reign and rule in peace and harmony as God's special possession. Sadly, this does not come to pass. Why? Because earthly kings are simply people with a propensity to sin. The entire Old Testament emphasizes this truth: God is good, but we mess it all up.

Lord, I don't want to participate in my own cycle of judges. I pray your Spirit within would reveal any hidden sin and shed light on attitudes and actions that don't honor you. Thank you for sending Jesus to break the sin cycle. I don't know what I'd do without you. Amen.

GOD IS A POET

○ **Morning:** Ruth 1–4
○ **Noon:** 1 Samuel 1–12
○ **Night:** Psalms 28–29

Did you know you can read the book of Ruth easily in one setting? You find that out today. Did you also know the story itself is a chiasm? A chiasm is an ancient way of storytelling in which the initial elements of the story have corresponding plot points at the end. In other words, what happens first is like what happens last. The narrative looks like the point of an arrow, where the top plot mirrors the bottom plot. At the center of the arrow is the main point of the chiasm. In the case of the book of Ruth, the central point is this: Boaz blesses Ruth's request and will begin to take steps to redeem her.

The chiastic structure is a literary device used throughout the Bible. It can be used in a verse, as in Genesis 9:6:

   (A) If anyone
     (B) Takes
       (C) A human life
       (C1) That person's life
     (B1) Will also be taken
   (A1) By human hands

Chiasm hunting is a really fun way to read the Bible. Here are some interesting ones to explore. (Note: Some are narrative, some are poetic, and others are instruction.)

- Genesis 11:1–9
- Exodus 31:13–17
- Leviticus 24:13–23
- Psalm 81
- Acts 6:1–7
- 1 Peter 1:2–21

Lord, thank you for the beautiful complexity of your Word. Thank you for providing a chiasm in the book of Ruth, pointing to redemption. Lord, I ask for strength and perseverance as I read your book rapidly. I want to understand it more. Please empower my understanding as I continue to read. Amen.

GOD RAISES UP A KING

○ **Morning:** 1 Samuel 13–16
○ **Noon:** 1 Samuel 17–24
○ **Night:** Psalm 30

The fulfillment of a calling takes a long time. And it's often fraught with obstacles and heartaches. Have you experienced this before?

When the nation of Israel demanded a king, Samuel the prophet acquiesced and gave them what they asked for—a broad-shouldered, seemingly capable, handsome leader named Saul. He is kingly and initially honors God with his position. But in chapter 15, we see his fickle heart, only partially obeying God, then justifying his lapse of obedience before Samuel. Samuel cries, "So because you have rejected the command of the LORD, he has rejected you as king" (1 Samuel 15:23).

This commenced the long, arduous calling of David. He was the runt of Jesse's tribe, tending sheep, when Samuel poured oil on his head. The Holy Spirit powerfully rested upon the boy, but he did not step into his kingship on that day; instead, it took fifteen more years to fulfill the calling.

Like Joseph—whose initial belief that he would rule came through his dreams as a teen, but whose leadership did not flourish until a lot of life had been lived—David had to walk through many dangers and trials before he would fulfill the calling on his life. This included an apprenticeship (his time with the sheep, with his lyre, and all those lonely, scary times as he protected sheep from predators), followed by his commissioning by Samuel. After that came years of testing, particularly when Saul, maddened, either loved David fiercely or chased him into caves, hunting his life. Pre-King David faced enemies, war, temptations, the wiles of the wilderness, giants, obscurity, pain, and constant fear. Many of David's best-loved songs no doubt came from this period of testing. We will experience his coronation in 2 Samuel 5 when he is thirty years old.

You can see this pattern throughout Scripture, but it's particularly poignant when we turn toward the New Testament and consider the life of Jesus. Although prophesied about as a baby, Jesus is thirty years old when he is anointed by the Holy Spirit through baptism. Immediately, he is thrust into isolating temptation in the wilderness. In this three-year ministry, he is constantly tested, experiencing conflict with the very ones who should herald him. His coronation happens at thirty-three, but his crown is not made of gold and precious gems—it is twisted from thorns.

Any calling the Lord brings involves sacrifice, testing, and lengthy periods of what Saint John of the Cross describes in his *Dark Night of the Soul*. These stories of real human beings waiting years to see their callings fulfilled are a necessary critique of our "I want it now" world. Be patient. Endure hardship. Fulfill your calling in your context, even if it's not everything you envisioned it to be.

Lord, thank you for your calling on my life. Help me be faithfully patient as you bring my ministry to fruition. I want to walk with integrity as I face any trials that come my way. More than anything, I know this is a journey. You are readying me for the next step. Help me to not grow discouraged as I wait. Amen.

GOD MAKES ANOTHER COVENANT

○ **Morning:** 1 Samuel 25–31
○ **Noon:** 2 Samuel 1–8
○ **Night:** Psalm 31

God creates holy agreements with humankind several times in the Old Testament. These are also known as covenants. A covenant is an agreement between a holy God and his people. It's either conditional (if you do this, then I will do that) or unconditional (no matter what you do, I will still do this).

You've already read about the Noahic Covenant: Upon flooding the entire earth, God promised to never do so again, the sign being a rainbow in the sky. This is an unconditional covenant, based on God's promise alone, and is not dependent on a holy nation.

In the Abrahamic Covenant God makes (and reiterates) with Abraham, God promises him offspring, a nation, and the land of Canaan. The sign of this covenant was circumcision.

The Mosaic Covenant (also known as the Old Covenant) was birthed on Mount Sinai, where God gave Moses the Ten Commandments, its sign being the practice of Sabbath every seventh day.

In Numbers 25, God makes a covenant with Phinehas also known as the Priestly Covenant. The faithfulness of Phinehas, the grandson of Aaron, spared the nation of Israel. God made a special covenant of peace with him and his descendants to be priests.

The fifth covenant God makes with David. In today's reading, God tells Nathan the prophet to relay important information to him. "But my favor will not be taken from him as I took it from

Saul, whom I removed from your sight. Your house and your kingdom will continue before me for all time, and your throne will be secure forever" (2 Samuel 7:15–16). The sign of this covenant was simply Solomon—the successor to the throne. In various places throughout the Old Testament, we read that God promises to be a Father to David (a shocking revelation) and that his kingship will be eternal (a seeming impossibility).

All these covenants are shadows or precursors, preparing God's people for what would become the New Covenant—an agreement no longer based on a stubborn people's obedience. The prophet Jeremiah hinted at the problem of the older covenants when he reminded, "This covenant will not be like the one I made with their ancestors when I took them by the hand and brought them out of the land of Egypt. They broke that covenant, though I loved them as a husband loves his wife" (Jeremiah 31:32). The New Covenant would be entirely different—an action enacted by God toward his people from the inside out. "I will put my instructions deep within them, and I will write them on their hearts. I will be their God, and they will be my people" (Jeremiah 31:33).

King Jesus was the fulfillment of the Davidic Covenant. He eternally reigns on a throne that is established forever. A descendent of David, Jesus fulfilled the covenant from both sides—as a human living a perfect life, and as God who always keeps his promises. Our God is a promise keeper!

> *Lord, thank you for keeping your agreements with us. Thank you even more for sending your Son to die in my place, to be a King forever who reigns and reigns and reigns. Because of that, I surrender afresh to you because you are mighty and good and beautiful. Amen.*

GOD EXPOSES SIN

○ **Morning:** 2 Samuel 9–16
○ **Noon:** 2 Samuel 17–21
○ **Night:** Psalms 32–33

We see the pinnacle of King David's reign at the beginning of today's reading. In 2 Samuel 10:19, peace comes to Israel. "When all the kings allied with Hadadezer saw that they had been defeated by Israel, they surrendered to Israel and became their subjects. After that, the Arameans were afraid to help the Ammonites."

But then everything turns awry.

During our reading today, we witness the fall of the house of David. One of the most important things we learn when we're reading the Bible briskly is to read the passage plainly, simply asking the basic journalistic questions of who, what, where, when, why, how. This is called observation.

So many people have wrongly interpreted Bathsheba as a temptress, but a plain reading of this passage reveals many stark realities:

- Bathsheba was most likely not naked as she bathed—the Scripture says she was washing from her monthly impurity.
- David would have known of her. She is the wife of one of his mighty fighting men, the daughter of another one of David's mighty men, and the granddaughter of Ahithophel, one of David's trusted advisors.
- She did not voluntarily go to the palace—she was taken by several men.
- There would have been no rescue for her—even if she screamed.

- David knew what he did was wrong, but instead of coming clean after finding out she was pregnant, he devised a devious plot to kill Bathsheba's husband.
- He married her (he had many wives, a clear violation of God's directive).
- Nathan the prophet never blames Bathsheba for the violation. He says, "You are that man!" (2 Samuel 12:7). All wrongdoing is leveled David's way.
- Even in the genealogies of Jesus, Bathsheba is still referred to as Uriah's wife (see Matthew 1:6).

Lord, I don't take this story lightly. And to be honest, it's frustrating to see someone so beloved of you fall from grace and harm so many people in the covering up of sin. Thank you that you still kept your promise, and that eventually in the narrative, a true King would reign forever who never, ever exploited anyone. Amen.

GOD IS IN TRANSITIONS

○ **Morning:** 2 Samuel 22–24
○ **Noon:** 1 Kings 1–10
○ **Night:** Psalm 34

Today we see the transition from King David to King Solomon, but before we do, David takes a moment to recount his legacy and praise his God. When we are walking through transitions, it's important we follow David's lead. Second Samuel 23 is the culmination of a kingdom that will eventually shift to a son, then to a divided kingdom. In short, nothing will ever be the same. Even so, David praised.

In 2 Samuel 22, he sang a song from the past, when God had proven his faithfulness by rescuing him from Saul and his enemies. "He rescued me from my powerful enemies, from those who hated me and were too strong for me. They attacked me at a moment when I was in distress, but the Lord supported me. He led me to a place of safety; he rescued me because he delights in me" (2 Samuel 22:18–20).

In looking back, David reminded himself of the power of God on his behalf. God had rescued him many times, and he chose to remember as many of God's mighty acts as he could. When you're walking through a transition from one job to another or one life stage to another, you can follow David's poetic example. Take some time today, if you have the bandwidth, to list the ways God has been faithful to you in the past. When did he deliver you from a terrible situation? When did he rescue you from yourself? How did he lead you to the place you are today? How did he protect you from harm? How did he reveal enemies in your life and strengthen you to fight them?

Such looking back not only helps you foster a heart of gratitude, but it also fortifies you for the next step of your transition. It grows your faith muscle.

In this case, David is transitioning from king to death. His last words reveal his heart. In chapter 23, he speaks of God and God alone. God is available. God communicates. God rules. God is light. God is a covenant-keeping God. God chooses people to do his work. God confirms every detail. God deals with enemies. God is to be feared.

Much is said these days about leadership and ministries and numbers as signs of faithfulness. But what if the marker of a true leader is simply acknowledging the greatness of God? What if it's not so much how you start your journey, but that you end it well? To finish well is a rare gift, and the Lord loves to empower you to do just that. As you stand on the threshold of transition, may it be your prayer to recount God's greatness and continue to be faithful to him in every life stage you face.

> *Lord, I pray I can finish well. But before I concentrate on that, help me transition well by recounting all the ways you have been faithful to me. Thank you for rescuing me, for giving me my life, for watching over me, for helping me when life got really hard. You are good. You are strong. You are worthy of my life. Amen.*

GOD GRIEVES DIVISIONS

○ **Morning:** 1 Kings 11–17
○ **Noon:** 1 Kings 18–22
○ **Night:** Psalm 35

We see the beauty and culmination of David's legacy when Solomon determines to build a masterpiece temple for the Lord. The nation of Israel experiences peace, and all seems well.

There are rumblings of problems, though.

While the wisdom of Solomon is legendary, his philandering and wayward heart as he chased after his many wives' gods eventually took over his legacy. When he passed away in 931 BC, the twelve tribes of Israel divided, beginning the era of the divided kingdom.

The godly stayed or fled to the Southern Kingdom where Jerusalem boasted temple worship and the priests maintained social and religious order. They were led by Solomon's son Rehoboam, who was somewhat faithful, but also chose not to tear down the places where the people worshiped idols. This kingdom in the south was known as Judah.

The Northern Kingdom, or Israel, is where ten of the twelve tribes remained, led by Jeroboam, son of Nebat. He was an apostate who worshiped foreign gods. When you read in the New Testament about Samaritans and Samaria, it is referring to this people and place. They constantly intermarried with other people, until their distinction as God's people faded away.

This divided kingdom is the backdrop for the prophets Elijah and Elisha.

You've probably heard of the king who reigned in the Northern Kingdom during the time of Elijah. Ahab was Israel's seventh king, reigning after his father, Omri. He married another famous person, Jezebel, the daughter of King Ethbaal of Sidon. You can see the word *baal* in her father's name, which means she certainly wasn't a God-fearer. She loved and worshiped Baal, the god of fertility who took on the form of a bull.

Ahab turned his back on his God. Not only that, but he also harmed his people. Together with Jezebel, they supported and promoted Baal's prophets.

That's when Elijah (his name means Jehovah is my God) has a crazy power encounter on Mount Carmel between him and the many prophets of Baal. We see a great demonstration of God's ability to consume a wet sacrifice, and the confirmation of God's power over the so-called Baal worshipers.

All that history culminates in this truth: Even in a divided, broken kingdom, God loved Israel so much that he sent a prophet to help them, to demonstrate his ability to lead, and to reorient them back toward their Creator. Even in the most hopeless, godless, evil times, God knows how to rescue and help the faithful. This is encouraging news.

We will be transitioning soon from the history books of the Bible to the major and minor prophets. The prophet's mandate was to help a soon-exiled Israel find their way back to God, and then prepare the way homeward, eventually culminating in the return of Israel to its land. This will set the stage for another Elijah—John the Baptist—to prepare the way for the Messiah of the world!

Lord, I know it breaks your heart when your people are divided and apostate. Even today there are divisions in your church. Please send messengers to help us find each other again. We don't want to worship foreign gods. We want to unify under our worship of you! Amen.

GOD PROVIDES A FORETASTE

○ **Morning:** 2 Kings 1–7
○ **Noon:** 2 Kings 8–14
○ **Night:** Psalm 36

The Bible is full of foreshadowing because it is an overarching story. And every good storyteller knows it's best to drop breadcrumbs along the way to entice the reader to keep reading. We see this in the prophet Elisha, Elijah's successor. He, too, is a prophet of miracles operating during the divided kingdom of Israel on the cusp of Israel's inevitable exile.

Elisha prophesied to the Northern Kingdom, a people with rulers tending toward apostasy and idol worship. Theirs was an affection toward Baal—worshiping him to the exclusion of the true God of Israel.

Baal was touted as controlling the elements, particularly water, so it's interesting to note that many of the miracles God did through Elisha involved water. He made undrinkable water potable near Jericho. An axe head floated miraculously, defying gravity's laws. God restored King Joram's water supply behind enemy lines.

Elisha was a hands-on prophet, tangibly meeting the needs of others, providing oil, a son, and healing to the people he met—often outsiders to Israel. This, again, revealed God's heart to bring everyone to himself, not simply the nation of Israel.

How does Elisha give us a foretaste? He is an archetype of Jesus, a hint at what will come.

Consider this: Elisha provided food (oil) to a widow in distress; Jesus provided food in the feeding of the 5,000 and 4,000 who would have had no sustenance had he not miraculously multiplied fish and loaves.

When the king of Aram asked the king of Israel to heal Naaman, it was Elisha who healed his leprosy. Similarly, a man with leprosy approached Jesus. "Jesus reached out and touched him. 'I am willing,' he said. 'Be healed!' And instantly the leprosy disappeared" (Matthew 8:3). Jesus even referred to Elisha's healing in Luke 4:27 when he was in Nazareth: "And many in Israel had leprosy in the time of the prophet Elisha, but the only one healed was Naaman, a Syrian." Why is this significant? Because Jesus is revealing to the people in Nazareth that God's kingdom does not merely consist of Israelites, but the entire world. Elisha's healing, therefore, is a foretaste of the coming kingdom under King Jesus, who would die on a cross to save the whole world.

In 2 Kings 4, we see an astounding miracle, of Elisha bringing back a child from death. This echoes what his predecessor Elijah did for the widow of Zarephath's son. Twice Jesus raises children from the dead. Interestingly, he also raises the son of Nain's widow, then Jairus's daughter. He is most famous for the raising of Lazarus in John chapter 11. So, we see foretastes of resurrection in the prophets, a fulfillment of resurrection throughout the ministry of Jesus, pointing to the ultimate resurrection of Jesus after his crucifixion. This is the immense beauty of the Bible—a cohesive, living story that builds to a powerful climax in the resurrection of Christ.

Lord, wow. Thank you. I am grateful for the foreshadowing I experienced today, how the prophets point me toward Jesus. Thank you for your Word. Thank you for the story of the Bible. Help me to uncover new connections as I read. Amen.

GOD IS SOVEREIGN

○ **Morning:** 2 Kings 15–20
○ **Noon:** 2 Kings 21–25
○ **Night:** Psalm 37

Throughout 1 and 2 Kings, we see the sovereignty of God in action. You probably see the word *sovereign* (king) in the word *sovereignty*, which means having supreme power or rule over a people or government. It has to do with ultimate ruling, royal rank, and dominion. In other words, to be sovereign is to be the greatest authority. God's sovereignty is a helpful fallback when the world spins crazily. Why? Because, as ruler and creator of all, God can be trusted to hold everything together.

We see this defined poetically by the apostle Paul in Colossians 1:15–17.

> Christ is the visible image of the invisible God.
>> He existed before anything was created and is supreme
>>> over all creation,
>> for through him God created everything
>>> in the heavenly realms and on earth.
>> He made the things we can see
>>> and the things we can't see—
>> such as thrones, kingdoms, rulers, and authorities in the
>>> unseen world.
>>> Everything was created through him and for him.
>> He existed before anything else,
>>> and he holds all creation together.

In today's reading we see God elevating some kings and deposing others. You might be tempted to think God's actions or inactions throughout this rebellious period in the nation of Israel's history are capricious, but they are not. Underneath it all is a proactive, purposeful God who is acting on behalf of his people. He allowed invaders to be agents of discipline for his rebellious children, only to relent and provide relief.

This sovereign God is not unmoved by our plight. His compassion is evident in the way he answers the prayers of the desperate. He hears Hezekiah's cries for Jerusalem, and he spares the leader's life as he faces sickness and death. Our sovereign God is moved by your prayers too. He is not detached from his people.

The Psalmist paints a beautiful picture of sovereignty in Psalm 135:5–6. "I know the greatness of the LORD—that our Lord is greater than any other god. The LORD does whatever pleases him throughout all heaven and earth, and on the seas and in their depths." Yes, God does whatever he pleases, but it pleases him to help those who love him.

Throughout Israel's history and the cycle of the judges we just experienced, you see this compassionate side of God's sovereignty. There's a nearly word-for-word repetition of Exodus 34:6 and Numbers 14:18 in Psalm 103:8: "The LORD is compassionate and merciful, slow to get angry and filled with unfailing love." Even when Israel acts unbecomingly, then suffers for waywardness, the Lord is moved by their plight and rescues them. Even as we move from Israel's deeper and deeper dive into idol worship toward exile, we will see this compassionate side of God emerge. This is good news. God's sovereign rule is not that of a detached, angry deity, but of a loving Father helping his children find true life.

Lord, thank you for your sovereignty. I'm grateful you are ruling this world with skill and intelligence. I'm also grateful for your mercy for Israel. It reminds me that you also have mercy for me. I so need your compassionate care today. Amen.

Day 28

GOD WARNS HIS PEOPLE

- **Morning:** Isaiah 1–9
- **Noon:** Isaiah 10–17
- **Night:** Psalms 38–39

You may be wondering why we've jumped ahead in your Bible reading today. We're doing that because we want to read the narrative as chronologically as possible. So, we're reading about the prophet who was alive immediately prior to and during the exile of the nation of Israel in the eighth century BC.

For context, Isaiah is the prophet during the reigns of Judah's kings Uzziah, Jothan, Ahaz, and Hezekiah. These kings ruled from Jerusalem at the end of the divided kingdom, prior to the exile to Babylon. All the kings, surprisingly, were good apart from Ahaz.

It's here that Isaiah warns the nation of the impending doom that will befall them. Because he remembers the goodness of God, he knows that God is full of mercy and will relent when Israel acknowledges its sin and repents.

Isaiah's warning language was twofold—containing both rebuke and hope. You'll see this in play throughout today's reading. Notice how Isaiah's words in 5:20–21 bend toward rebuke: "What sorrow for those who say that evil is good and good is evil, that dark is light and light is dark, that bitter is sweet and sweet is bitter. What sorrow for those who are wise in their own eyes and think themselves so clever." His words are both timely and timeless—timely in that the nation was truly calling evil good, but also timelessly universal in that we are seeing the same phenomenon today. This is the incisiveness of God's Word, able to exegete the moment as well as our current context.

Later, in Isaiah 16:4–5, we see hope emerge. "When oppression and destruction have ended and enemy raiders have disappeared, then God will establish one of David's descendants as king. He will rule with mercy and truth. He will always do what is just and be eager to do what is right." Jesus is the fulfillment of Isaiah's words (and interestingly, Isaiah is the most quoted prophet in the New Testament).

In John 1:14, we see those same qualities of mercy and truth residing in Jesus. "And the Word became flesh and dwelt among us, and we have seen his glory, glory as of the only Son from the Father, full of grace and truth" (ESV).

Remember, the Old Testament is a signaler of what would come later. It is the beginning of the chiastic structure of the Bible, where the fall of humankind, judgment, nation building, and exile will hinge on the fulcrum of the life of Jesus, followed by the inclusion of humanity in the church, kingdom building, judgment at the end of time, and the restoration of all things in the New Heavens and the New Earth. Isaiah's words point toward that coming reality.

Lord, thank you for warnings. Thank you for hope. Thank you that you're the fulcrum of the change that is to come, where you will restore all the things we messed up in our sin. I confess I'm weary of the pain of this world. Please hold me as I wait for your glorious Next! Amen.

✓ Day 29

GOD REBUKES AND ENCOURAGES

○ **Morning:** Isaiah 18–25
○ **Noon:** Isaiah 26–35
○ **Night:** Psalm 40

As mentioned yesterday, Isaiah's warnings to Israel have hope infused in them. J. R. R. Tolkien coined a word about this kind of language in *eucatastrophe*. It means a surprising, happy turn of events. Tolkien writes, "In such stories when the sudden 'turn' comes we get a piercing glimpse of joy, and heart's desire, that for a moment passes outside the frame, rends indeed the very web of story, and lets a gleam come through."[1]

We see the turning of Isaiah's remarks in the last chapter of today's reading, Isaiah 35. Look at his phraseologies about what will come to Israel in the future:

- "Even the wilderness and desert will be glad in those days" (v. 1).

- "Be strong, and do not fear, for your God is coming to destroy your enemies. He is coming to save you" (v. 4).

- "He will open the eyes of the blind and unplug the ears of the deaf" (v. 5). Do you see Jesus in these verses?

- "The lame will leap like a deer, and those who cannot speak will sing for joy!" (v. 6). Again, we see a hinting at what Jesus would do—heal the lame and restore the deaf and mute.

- "And a great road will go through that once deserted land. It will be named the Highway of Holiness" (v. 8).

- "Sorrow and mourning will disappear, and they will be filled with joy and gladness" (v. 10).

The Bible has a telescoping quality about it, speaking to the direct cultural context, hinting at the next stage in history, and foretelling the end and beginning of all things—something we'll see gloriously fulfilled in Revelation 21. One day there will be no more catastrophes. There will be only good as God dwells forever with his people (us!) in harmony, in a new world no longer tainted by the ravages of sin.

As a prophet, Isaiah saw all this restoration from afar, as if he looked on tiptoes at the coming beautification of all things. His rebuke would be laced with encouragement because this world is not what it seems. There is more. And we are made for more. Can you see it? Can you taste it? Someday you will be wholly whole, vibrantly alive, and dearly loved—all because of the God who brings goodness from catastrophe.

Lord, thanks for eucatastrophe, that you bring beauty from difficulties, life from death, hope from despair. When I am discouraged, would you prompt me to remember how things will be in the next life? I long to be set free from sin. I long to see you face-to-face. Amen.

GOD PRAISES HIS SERVANT

○ **Morning:** Isaiah 36–41
○ **Noon:** Isaiah 42–48
○ **Night:** Psalm 41

You are now a third of the way through the Bible! Can you believe it? I'm so proud of your tenacity, and my prayer is that you are falling in love with the beauty and power of God's Word. There is so much treasure here!

Today we meet what's commonly known as the Suffering Servant. There's paradox to this surprising biblical figure. Many times, the Suffering Servant is Israel. You see this throughout Isaiah chapter 41. You hear God's affection toward Israel here: "When the poor and needy search for water and there is none, and their tongues are parched from thirst, then I, the LORD, will answer them. I, the God of Israel, will never abandon them" (v. 17).

But the Suffering Servant is also portrayed as a kingly person who loves to help those who are broken. There are four songs about this servant in chapters 42, 49, 50, and 52. He is obedient, and he suffers for the sake of others. Remind you of anyone? You can see the harmony of this idea because Jesus himself confirms he is the Suffering Servant. (We'll look at this on Day 32.)

We see a powerful link between Isaiah 42:2–4 and Matthew 12:17–21 where Matthew quotes the ancient passage, giving those who hear a poignant reminder that Jesus is the fulfillment of the Suffering Servant.

This fulfilled the prophecy of Isaiah concerning him:

"Look at my Servant, whom I have chosen.
He is my Beloved, who pleases me.

I will put my Spirit upon him,
    and he will proclaim justice to the nations.
He will not fight or shout
    or raise his voice in public.
He will not crush the weakest reed
    or put out a flickering candle.
Finally he will cause justice to be victorious.
And his name will be the hope of all the world."

As you read about the Suffering Servant, you'll find many uncanny parallels to the life of Jesus, particularly as Jesus loved outsiders and the broken in his midst. In reference to the Matthew passage above, we do know Jesus had the very Spirit of God indwelling him. We know that Jesus had a heart for justice, not merely for his country Israel, but for the whole world. After all, he laid down his life for everyone. In public, other than turning over the tables in the temple when confronting religious abuse, he was gentle, kindhearted, and conciliatory. And he often healed the broken of mind, body, and spirit.

We're reminded here that Jesus and his name are truly the hope of the world. The Old Testament beautifully points us toward him, and he is the centrality of our faith. If we want to be like him, it helps when we study his predicted attributes as we read about the Suffering Servant. We will uncover his patience, his longing for justice for those oppressed, his heart for humankind, and his tenacity through suffering. While Israel was expecting a victorious messiah to politically deliver them from foreign oppression, they missed the very strong hints in Isaiah that their messiah would suffer.

Lord, thank you for so perfectly fulfilling Scripture. I'm grateful to see how your Word interacts with itself in the Old and New Testaments. Thank you for suffering for my sake, for the world's sake. Thank you for sending Jesus to this broken world. Amen.

GOD BRINGS EXODUS

○ **Morning:** Isaiah 49–55
○ **Noon:** Isaiah 56–60
○ **Night:** Psalms 42–43

When you hear the word *exodus*, you most likely conjure up images of the Red Sea parting in dynamic fashion. You think of the plagues in Egypt, a plucky yet reluctant prophet Moses, and the ability of God to deliver a people from a nation stronger. And you'd be right.

But have you considered God loves exodus, and he enacts it a second time here?

Many call the return from exile, from Babylon back to a ruined Jerusalem, the second exodus. The past exodus is one of the themes of the book of Isaiah, so as you continue reading it, do so with that in mind. You may uncover new treasure.

When Israel is commanded to return, their exodus must involve repentance—leaving behind what brought on their captivity in the first place. "Get out! Get out and leave your captivity, where everything you touch is unclean. Get out of there and purify yourselves, you who carry home the sacred objects of the LORD" (Isaiah 52:11).

If you go back to Isaiah 43, you'll see that God tells them this new exodus will be different. In verses 15–17, God reminds the nation of the past exodus, helping them remember that he was the initiator of the deliverance through the Red Sea and performed the miraculous on their behalf.

Then the narrative takes a turn with the word *but* as it continues in verses 18–19. "But forget all that—it is nothing compared to what I am going to do. For I am about to do something new. See, I have already begun! Do you not see it? I will make a pathway through the wilderness. I will create rivers in the dry wasteland." On their exodus from Babylon to Jerusalem, God will guide them through the wilderness (rather than the Red Sea). And instead of damming up rivers and seas, he will create water from dust.

In this new deliverance, God will feed them. "They will neither hunger nor thirst. The searing sun will not reach them anymore. For the LORD in his mercy will lead them; he will lead them beside cool waters" (Isaiah 49:10).

He will guide and protect them on this second exodus. "The LORD will guide you continually, giving you water when you are dry and restoring your strength. You will be like a well-watered garden, like an ever-flowing spring" (Isaiah 58:11).

He will utterly transform their circumstances from desolation to joy. "The Lord will comfort Israel again and have pity on her ruins. Her desert will blossom like Eden, her barren wilderness like the garden of the LORD. Joy and gladness will be found there. Songs of thanksgiving will fill the air" (Isaiah 51:3).

Lord, in reading about this second exodus, I realize I need one too. Would you provide it for me? Would you lead me near cool waters—my soul is parched. Would you restore my strength? Would you change my pain to joy? I trust you to do all this. Amen.

GOD FULFILLS PROPHECY

○ **Morning:** Isaiah 61–66
○ **Noon:** Hosea 1–14
○ **Night:** Psalm 44

You've most likely read Isaiah 61:1–2 before, or perhaps you remember hearing it come from Jesus's mouth. He quotes most of it in Luke 4:18–19 when he begins his ministry. To set the stage, he has just walked through the temptation in the wilderness and has returned to Galilee, to Nazareth, where he grew up.

Jesus steps into his hometown synagogue, unrolls the scroll of the prophet Isaiah, and reads, "The Spirit of the LORD is upon me, for he has anointed me to bring Good News to the poor. He has sent me to proclaim that captives will be released, that the blind will see, that the oppressed will be set free, and that the time of the LORD's favor has come." Imagine what people were thinking as he read! This is a clear reference to the Suffering Servant we discussed two days ago.

The Scripture continues, "He rolled up the scroll, handed it back to the attendant, and sat down. All eyes in the synagogue looked at him intently. Then he began to speak to them. 'The Scripture you've just heard has been fulfilled this very day!'" (Luke 4:20–21).

First, take note that Jesus sits down. This is symbolic of fulfillment. When you finish a task, you sit down. When Jesus ascended to the Father, he sat down, having done all he'd been tasked to do. "When the Lord Jesus had finished talking with them, he was taken up into heaven and sat down in the place of honor at God's right hand" (Mark 16:19).

Jesus clearly told the hometown crowd that this simple carpenter from within their ranks had far more to him than they had realized. By equating himself with the Suffering Servant, he told them he was the fulfillment of Scripture, revealing himself as their promised messiah without coming out and saying it directly. Those who knew the Scriptures well would have been quickened and possibly perplexed.

Even more telling is what Jesus didn't read. He left out a sentence from verse two. He ends with God's favor, but doesn't read, "and with it, the day of God's anger against their enemies" (Isaiah 61:2). Why?

Two possible reasons.

One: He did not want the nation of Israel to think he was coming as a military dictator, a triumphant king who would vanquish Israel's oppressor Rome. That would be too shortsighted, and certainly did not pertain to his initial mission on earth. He came to seek and save the lost, not to kill people who held power over Israel. The power he would subdue was much deeper, more insidious—the power of hell itself.

Two: He would fulfill the latter part of verse two at the end of time. He allowed the comma to be a period for the time being. There would come a time of divine judgment when all the wrongs would be righted, but it was not that day.

> *Lord, I'm astounded at the beauty of Scripture, how you perfectly fulfilled it, and how you will continue to do so in the age to come. Thank you for completing the work you intended to do on the cross. Thank you for delivering me from the domain of darkness to your marvelous light! Amen.*

GOD CALLS US BACK

○ **Morning:** Joel 1–3
○ **Noon:** Amos 1–9 and Obadiah 1
○ **Night:** Psalms 45–46

You are reading the minor prophets now. They're also known as the Twelve Prophets: Hosea, Joel, Amos, Obadiah, Jonah, Micah, Nahum, Habakkuk, Zephaniah, Haggai, Zechariah, and Malachi. They're named *minor* not because of ranking or importance, but because each of these books is shorter than the major prophets like Isaiah, Jeremiah (who also wrote Lamentations), Ezekiel, and Daniel.

These prophets have a consistent message of prophesying against idolatry, predicting the exile, and offering encouragement for the nation when they return from exile. But underneath all this is a persistent calling to return to the One who created them.

Yesterday you read in Hosea about a prophet who embodied the heartache of God by marrying a prostitute as a demonstration of Israel's fickle idolatry. He ends his time by writing, "O Israel, stay away from idols! I am the one who answers your prayers and cares for you. I am like a tree that is always green; all your fruit comes from me" (Hosea 14:8). Can you hear the longing of God in those verses? He desired to woo a rebellious nation back to himself.

The prophet Amos repeats a refrain in chapter 4 that is haunting, in verses 6, 8, 9, 10, and 11: "But still you would not return to me." Though the Lord brought discipline, deprivation, crop failures, plagues, and destruction because of their idolatry and affection for other gods, particularly Baal, they never seemed to take the hint and return.

He goes on to malign the leaders of Israel. "I hate all your show and pretense—the hypocrisy of your religious festivals and solemn assemblies. . . . Away with your noisy hymns of praise! I will not listen to the music of your harps" (Amos 5:21, 23).

What does the Lord want? Their return. Their repentance. Their hearts. Their righteous actions that flow from compassion. "Instead, I want to see a mighty flood of justice, an endless river of righteous living" (Amos 5:24).

The remainder of the book is an indictment of the nation, detailing the doom that will come if they choose not to return.

Thankfully, there is hope. As we've been learning, our God is slow to anger—even when his people rebel and turn away from him. Amos reminds the people of Israel that God will repair them, restore the glory of Jerusalem, and reestablish their agricultural bounty. God promises, "I will firmly plant them there in their own land. They will never again be uprooted from the land I have given them" (Amos 9:15).

Isn't it interesting that when God brings restoration, garden imagery emerges? We're all longing for our perfect home, the Garden of Eden, and restoration looks an awful lot like returning to Paradise. We'll see this idea of a return to Eden throughout the Scriptures, so pay attention every time you see positive agricultural references.

Lord, thank you that you long to be in relationship with me, that you beckon me to return to you, to seek you, to forsake the idols in my life for the beauty of following you. Would you restore the garden of my life? Bring flourishing and fruit, I pray. Amen.

GOD LOVES EVERYONE—EVEN NINEVITES!

- ○ **Morning:** Jonah 1–4
- ○ **Noon:** Micah 1–7 and Nahum 1–3
- ○ **Night:** Psalms 47–48

Today's reading has two different outcomes for Israel's hated enemies, the Ninevites. Between Jonah and Nahum there's a span of a hundred years. In Jonah's case, we see the Ninevites turn from their wickedness, but in Nahum's later account, their "repentance" had not lasted the century, and they are destroyed.

Even so, we see the missionary heartbeat of God, particularly in the book of Jonah. This book, though prophetic and included in the minor prophets, is entirely different because it's written in narrative form. In other words, it tells a story.

The story takes place in the Northern Kingdom of Israel (during the divided kingdom). You may recall that the Northern Kingdom struggled to follow God because they were often prone to worship Baal. However, the current king, Jeroboam II, did have military and political success despite the nation's continued fickle heart toward the things of God. During this time, the creep of the other nations wanting to oppress and overthrow Israel lessened. This is the setting of Jonah. God asked him to preach in Nineveh, the capital of Assyria, when the Assyrians' strength was waning for a period.

The book falls into two parts: when God asks Jonah to go (and Jonah runs the other way), and when Jonah reluctantly preaches to the Ninevites and sees a crazy revival result—much to his crabby chagrin. Like the book of Ruth, Jonah is told in a chiastic structure, where what happens in the beginning is echoed in the end. The fulcrum upon which the chiasm hinges is the recommissioning of Jonah. "Then the LORD spoke to Jonah a second time. 'Get up and go to the great city of Nineveh, and deliver the message I have given you'" (Jonah 3:1–2).

Jonah, as you remember, gladly foretells of the doom that will befall Israel's archenemies. You can almost hear his glee, anticipating the judgment of God. But alas! It is not to be because the whole country repents.

Here is where we see God's great compassion for the lost. Jonah bitterly complains about God's mercy when he says, "Didn't I say before I left home that you would do this, LORD? That is why I ran away to Tarshish! I knew that you are a merciful and compassionate God, slow to get angry and filled with unfailing love. You are eager to turn back from destroying people" (Jonah 4:2).

God's plan, as you've been experiencing the past four weeks, has always been to bring all people to himself. Although Israel is special in his eyes, he chose them to be a beacon to the whole world. Reach one country, and, through them, reach the world. But Israel's continued prejudice against other nations darkened them from longing to see a world reconciled to their Creator.

Lord, I want to have a missionary heartbeat like yours. Expose the parts of me that are blind to your mercy. Show me where I've failed to love those who are different from me. I want to be more intentional about my prayers for the lost. Amen.

✓ Day 35

GOD WELCOMES AUTHENTICITY

○ **Morning:** Habakkuk 1–3 and Zephaniah 1–3
○ **Noon:** Job 1–7
○ **Night:** Psalms 49–50

You've read two books of the Bible today and started one of the most difficult ones. Well done, good and faithful Bible reader!

In the book of Habakkuk, you may have noticed the minor prophet's frustration with God. He asks the age-old question, "How long, O LORD, must I call for help?" (Habakkuk 1:2). He then complains about the state of his country, the violence surrounding him, and the lack of justice he's experiencing. (Sound familiar? There's nothing new under the sun!)

What Habakkuk does is lament. He knows God's shoulders are big enough to carry his complaints. And God does not chastise Habakkuk for his honesty—he listens. When God answers, it's not necessarily how Habakkuk would've wanted it (God would use evil Babylon to chastise Israel).

Have you ever felt that way? That when you're walking through a difficult time, another difficult thing happens?

Lament takes on a specific structure, typically. It starts with authentic complaint, then morphs into a confession of trust in the middle of the current conundrum, followed by a request that God would intervene. After that, the lamenter chooses to praise God during their current pain, and then reminds himself or herself that God is in control.

The entire book of Habakkuk is a lament like this. It's beautifully summarized in a popular Old Testament passage.

> I trembled inside when I heard this;
> my lips quivered with fear.

My legs gave way beneath me,
    and I shook in terror.
I will wait quietly for the coming day
    when disaster will strike the people who invade us.
Even though the fig trees have no blossoms,
    and there are no grapes on the vines;
even though the olive crop fails,
    and the fields lie empty and barren;
even though the flocks die in the fields,
    and the cattle barns are empty,
yet I will rejoice in the LORD!
    I will be joyful in the God of my salvation!
The Sovereign LORD is my strength!
    He makes me as surefooted as a deer,
    able to treat upon the heights.

Habakkuk 3:16–19

God does not despise our authenticity about a painful situation—he redeems it. He has created a way for us to process our grief and bewilderment through honest lament. We will see a lot of this as we make our way through the book of Job. Job is known as an honest, God-fearing man who experiences many, many trials. In that godliness, he shares his pain with God. Even though his friends chastise him for doing so, he continues to process his grief out loud.

Unprocessed grief (the kind we stuff) tends to come back and haunt us later. This is why it's so amazing that God welcomes our questions, worries, fears, and pain. He can handle our confusion. He can carry our anger.

Lord, thank you that you are big enough to shoulder my anger, questions, and pain. Thank you that Habakkuk reminds me that even when things are decidedly not going my way, I can still exercise trust and faith in you. Help me to praise you through my grief today. Amen.

✓ Day 36

GOD REIGNS OVER DEATH

○ **Morning:** Job 8–16
○ **Noon:** Job 17–23
○ **Night:** Psalm 51

There's a beautiful passage about the afterlife tucked inside the pain Job is experiencing. As you know, God allowed Satan to bring trial upon trial into Job's life. And initially, Job responded quite surprisingly. "I came naked from my mother's womb, and I will be naked when I leave. The LORD gave me what I had, and the LORD has taken it away. Praise the name of the LORD!" (Job 1:21). Here he hints at the afterlife—that we cannot bring our stuff with us.

But as he continues this painful journey and curses the day of his birth, counselors come into his life and begin judging him relentlessly. One of these friends, Bildad, reminds Job in chapter 18 that God judges wicked people in the same way he judged Job, basically equating Job with wickedness.

Chapter 19 is Job's response. After asking his friends to please have mercy on him (vv. 21–22), Job seems to break into song. "But as for me, I know that my Redeemer lives, and he will stand upon the earth at last. And after my body has decayed, yet in my body I will see God! I will see him for myself. Yes, I will see him with my own eyes. I am overwhelmed at the thought!" (vv. 25–27).

The Hebrew word for redeemer is *go'el,* and it is used in both civil and criminal contexts. You could redeem property or avenge bloodshed—it's the same idea. When you read the book of Ruth, you met Boaz, the kinsman-redeemer who basically purchased Ruth's lot in life, securing a legacy for her mother-in-law Naomi. To redeem is to change the state of, to bring back to life.

To realize how surprising Job's use of this term is, as well as his insisting on seeing God after death, we must look at a typical Jewish person's concept of the afterlife. Throughout the Old Testament, when you die, it's a dire situation—you go to a dark, dismal place, often called *Sheol*, or a pit full of death (*Shakhat*). Or they simply call it *Qeber*, the grave.

But also in the Old Testament there are hints of something different when it comes to the afterlife. David wrote, "You will show me the way of life, granting me the joy of your presence and the pleasures of living with you forever" (Psalm 16:11). The verse prior says, "For you will not leave my soul among the dead or allow your holy one to rot in the grave" (Psalm 16:10). This is the very verse the apostle Paul quotes, applying it to Jesus's resurrection in Acts 13:35.

So, when Job speaks of a Redeemer, he could be telescoping into the future, when a messiah would redeem his people, not merely with a legal contract, but with his life, death, and resurrection.

Lord, you are my Redeemer, the one who has snatched me from the clutches of the grave and brought me abundant life. Thank you. I'm grateful that I won't be subjected to dusty, scary Sheol, but that when I die, I'll see you. Amen.

GOD IS WISE

○ **Morning:** Job 24–30
○ **Noon:** Job 31–37
○ **Night:** Psalms 52–53

We often speak of God's power and might, but perhaps we forget to meditate on his amazing intelligence and wisdom. In comparison to our wisdom, his soars above. Tomorrow we'll begin an entire book dedicated to the wisdom of God, the book of Proverbs, where we'll see all the facets of God's wisdom on display.

But tucked into the book of Job are two very interesting chapters that discuss wisdom. In chapter 27, Job chronicles the so-called wisdom of the wicked. In short, it's not pretty. The wicked person's wisdom leads them toward destruction.

What follows in chapter 28 is a song Job sings about the wisdom of God and how difficult it is to find it as a human being. "But do people know where to find wisdom? Where can they find understanding? No one knows where to find it, for it is not found among the living. . . . It is hidden from the eyes of all humanity. Even the sharp-eyed birds in the sky cannot discover it" (vv. 12–13, 21).

We learn wisdom's value—that it is more expensive than the finest gold, greater in value than lapis lazuli, more beautiful than jewels, more costly than rubies (see 28:15–19.) So, if it is unattainable to the wicked, difficult to find for common humanity, more valuable than anything the earth can produce, how in the world can we find it?

Job answers simply.

"God alone understands the way to wisdom; he knows where it can be found, for he looks throughout the whole earth and sees everything under the heavens" (28:23–24).

God is wise. He is the creator of wisdom. In his wisdom he created everything we see. He understands physics (he created physics!). He knows the intricacies of the human heart (even we cannot understand our own hearts!). He controls the weather. He protects the innocent. He clothes the lilies of the field. He chases after the broken. He knows all mysteries. He has all knowledge.

If we want and need wisdom, we must turn to him. He is the source of it all.

At the end of the chapter, Job puts words in God's mouth—about wisdom. "And this is what he says to all humanity: 'The fear of the Lord is true wisdom; to forsake evil is real understanding'" (Job 28:28).

The pathway toward wisdom, then, is twofold. We first must revere God for his powerful otherness. We can't do this life on our own, relying on our paltry, small wisdom. Second, we must turn away from evil. When we do that, we are turning toward the One who is good, and in that circle of relationship, God generously gives us the wisdom we need to live and move and breathe.

Lord, I realize that in my own wisdom, I have difficulties. Instead, I choose to fear you—the source of all wisdom. Help me to seek you first in everything, and, in that, turn away from the things that would captivate my soul. Pour your wisdom into me today, I pray. Amen.

GOD IS SEEN

○ **Morning:** Job 38–42
○ **Noon:** Proverbs 1–3
○ **Night:** Psalms 54–55

We see quite a transformation throughout the book of Job—a difficult book to digest. Known by most scholars as the most ancient Old Testament book written, the story plays out in dynamic detail of a man who deeply loved God, a bargain struck (undergirded in God's sovereignty) with the devil, and the inevitable fallout of grief.

You may have noticed that the book begins in block prose—to set up the story—but most of the remainder of the book is written in stanzas of poetry. Sometimes grief and pain can only be processed that way, with rhythm and a poetic bent toward handling pain. Again, the book resolves when God vindicates Job in prose.

Though they began well when they first approached Job (empathetically sat with him in his grief), we see Job's friends offer him platitudes and clichés for the rest of the book, particularly bent on blaming righteous Job for the circumstances that befell him. Have you ever had this happen? When you were walking through the valley of grief, did someone fill the air, not with quiet empathy, but with words of "helpful" advice tinged with judgment? We learn exactly how God feels about "friends" like these. God indicts them when addressing Eliphaz. "I am angry with you and your two friends, for you have not spoken accurately about me, as my servant Job has" (Job 42:7).

Job, no doubt, was harmed by his friends, but the Lord did not want him to stay in that state of bitterness. His restoration was completed only *after* he prayed for his friends—an act of forgiveness and reconciliation. "When Job prayed for his friends, the LORD restored his fortunes" (Job 42:10).

The last bit of poetry in the book, before the paragraphs telling of Job's restoration, is a decree made by Job that is particularly instructive. While we so desperately want harmony and peace in our lives, it's often suffering and difficulties that cause us to know more of God. When we walk through pain, we initially may blame the Lord, but inevitably we reach for him, and we find him to be faithful and present. Job writes, "I had only heard about you before, but now I have seen you with my own eyes" (Job 42:5).

Job begins his suffering journey knowing *about* God, but not truly knowing him. At the end of his journey, before God restores his fortunes, Job *sees* God. What a powerful testimony to the way God works even the most horrific circumstances for our good!

Lord, while I don't court disaster, and I'm not fond of pain, I am grateful for the way you skillfully transform difficult situations into my better character, for your great glory. You are so amazing to work in and through my suffering. Thank you. Amen.

GOD CARES ABOUT OUR DAILY LIVES

○ **Morning:** Proverbs 4–8
○ **Noon:** Proverbs 9–15
○ **Night:** Psalms 56–57

The book of Proverbs is a practical book. Now that you're rapid-reading it, you probably understand that truth even more. Many verses speak of obeying parents, searching for wisdom as if it were gold, running away from adultery, managing our finances well, and establishing a strong work ethic.

But today I want to focus on daily habits. What kind of habits does a wise person practice? In these couplets you'll find both a positive example and its opposite—sort of a rah-rah to do right and a cautionary tale about doing wrong.

Wise people speak life. In every situation, they find ways to encourage the people in their lives. "The words of the godly are a life-giving fountain; the words of the wicked conceal violent intentions" (Proverbs 10:11).

Wise people practice honesty. They tell the truth even when it hurts them. "The godly are directed by honesty; the wicked fall beneath their load of sin" (Proverbs 11:5).

Wise people welcome discipline and correction because they know they cannot grow without it. This means they are open to living in community with others. (How can you be corrected if you have no one in your life?) "To learn, you must love discipline; it is stupid to hate correction" (Proverbs 12:1).

Wise people have a strong work ethic because they know it honors God to be good stewards of the gifts he's given them. "Work hard and become a leader; be lazy and become a slave" (Proverbs 12:24).

Wise people choose to harness their tongues. Instead of spouting everything they think or feel, they've learned the important lesson of restraint, particularly in volatile conversations. "Those who control their tongue will have a long life; opening your mouth can ruin everything" (Proverbs 13:3).

Wise people practice peace in their relationships, forsaking bitterness, jealousy, and contention. "A peaceful heart leads to a healthy body; jealousy is like cancer in the bones" (Proverbs 14:30).

While the Bible is not merely a manual for life (it is so much more), it's heartening to see such practical advice in its pages, don't you think?

> *Lord, thank you for teaching me today about good habits. Help me to honor you with my lips, my work ethic, and my willingness to be corrected. I do want daily peace in my relationships, and I see now that harmony is often tied up in my responses (or my choice not to respond). Amen.*

GOD IS INTERESTED IN OUR FINANCES

○ **Morning:** Proverbs 16–21
○ **Noon:** Proverbs 22–27
○ **Night:** Psalms 58–59

The book of Proverbs offers much advice about how we are to handle our finances. It speaks of wealth, the wealthy, poverty, and the poor. While there may be general principles of wealth (if you are godly, wealth can come; if you are lazy, wealth may flee), Proverbs also deals in nuance.

What can we learn from today's reading?

We must be content, truth-telling people, no matter what we have. "Better to have little, with godliness, than to be rich and dishonest" (Proverbs 16:8).

We must be fair. "The LORD demands accurate scales and balances; he sets the standards for fairness" (Proverbs 16:11).

We must be mindful of the poor among us and treat each person with dignity and respect. "Those who mock the poor insult their Maker; those who rejoice at the misfortune of others will be punished" (Proverbs 17:5).

We must practice rigorous honesty. "Better to be poor and honest than to be dishonest and a fool" (Proverbs 19:1).

We are to be generous with those who have less. "If you help the poor, you are lending to the LORD—and he will repay you" (Proverbs 19:17).

We pay our debts. "Just as the rich rule the poor, so the borrower is servant to the lender" (Proverbs 22:7).

We don't co-sign a loan. "Don't agree to guarantee another person's debt or put up security for someone else. If you can't pay it, even your bed will be snatched from under you" (Proverbs 22:26–27).

We don't chase riches, and we understand their fickle nature. "Don't wear yourself out trying to get rich. Be wise enough to know when to quit. In the blink of an eye wealth disappears, for it will sprout wings and fly away like an eagle" (Proverbs 23:4–5).

We keep our financial promises. "A person who promises a gift but doesn't give it is like clouds and wind that bring no rain" (Proverbs 25:14).

> Lord, I want to honor you with my finances. Thank you for such wise, sound advice! Help me to be wise, generous, and frugal. I want to be a good steward of all you've given me. I understand you own it all anyway, but I want to honor you as I live and give. Amen.

GOD WANTS US TO ENJOY

○ **Morning:** Proverbs 28–31
○ **Noon:** Ecclesiastes 1–12
○ **Night:** Psalms 60–61

Congratulations! Today you're reading through one of the Bible's most difficult-to-understand books, Ecclesiastes! Hopefully you don't feel that your life is meaningless.

The Hebrew word translated "meaningless" in Ecclesiastes 1:2 is *hebel*. The word means taking a deep breath, or it can mean vapor, like a mist that disappears once the sun rises. It's meant to connote brevity. Jesus hints at this when he says, "And if God cares so wonderfully for flowers that are here today and thrown into the fire tomorrow, he will certainly care for you. Why do you have so little faith?" (Luke 12:28).

Hebel is the opposite of *glory*, which means to give weight to or heaviness in worth. In contrast, *hebel* is light and airy, with no sure foundation. There are several ways to translate the word in different languages. In Greek, translators used *mataiotes*, a word that means futile or empty. In the Latin Vulgate, the word is translated *vanitas*, where you can clearly see the word *vanity*. In reading this word, we're meant to feel the pointlessness or aimlessness or futility.

All that to say, we instinctively know life is fleeting, don't we? That's why the author of Ecclesiastes (an editor who highlighted Solomon's words) admonishes us that it's "better to spend your time at funerals than at parties. After all, everyone dies—so the living should take this to heart. Sorrow is better than laughter, for sadness has a refining influence on us" (Ecclesiastes 7:2–3). When we realize the brevity of life, we tend to live it better, making the most of the fleeting time we have.

The summary of this book, besides the paramount importance of fearing God above all, is, ironically, enjoyment. Because we know the seemingly purposeless nature of our quick-as-a-vapor life, it is right and good to enjoy what God has given us—to steep ourselves in the good gifts he gives. "And it is a good thing to receive wealth from God and the good health to enjoy it. To enjoy your work and accept your lot in life—this is indeed a gift from God. God keeps such people so busy enjoying life that they take no time to brood over the past" (Ecclesiastes 5:19–20).

This fits hand in glove with the Bible's recommendation for feasting. "So go ahead. Eat your food with joy, and drink your wine with a happy heart, for God approves of this!" (Ecclesiastes 9:7).

God wants us to enjoy what he has given us, with a happy, discerning heart, knowing that each day like that is a gift, from his hands to our hearts.

> *Lord, help me to feast! Even amid understanding my own frailty on this earth and the brevity of life, help me understand how to live life to its fullest, to consider enjoyment a spiritual discipline. Thank you for including this book in your Word. Amen.*

GOD IS PRO-POETRY

○ **Morning:** Song of Solomon 1–8
○ **Noon:** Jeremiah 1–6
○ **Night:** Psalms 62–63

Have you ever read the Song of Solomon in one sitting? This book is a collection of poetry, and it's meant to be read from cover to cover. The book is a series of dialogues in poetic form written primarily from the perspective of a woman.

There are three ways this book has traditionally been interpreted, two allegorical and one at face value.

First, Jewish scholars see this as an allegory in which the woman represents Israel, and the man represents God. What follows is a story about God's deep love for his people.

Second, Christian scholars also see the book as allegorical, but now they rely heavily on Paul's teaching about marriage and how it represents Christ and the church in Ephesians 5:25–33. In this case, the woman is the Bride of Christ, and Christ is the bridegroom.

Third, because of recent archeological excavations that unearthed similar love poetry, the most recent interpretation is that this book is simply a collection of love poems.

However you interpret the book, the stark fact remains that this is a book about romantic love, the joy of attraction, and the power of seeking and finding. You see a lot of push and pull in this book, of losing a lover, only to find the lover—and all the angsty stress involved in pursuit.

You also may have noticed a lot of imagery around creation—particularly about gardens. Taken with Genesis in mind, this should link you back to the place where romantic, intimate love blossomed. The first couple lived in an idyllic place. They were naked, yet unashamed. In light of this hint at Eden, one thing we can take away from this book of poetry is that God is in the business of restoring everything—creation, humankind, and even human love.

We begin the Bible in a garden. We see the land of Israel in similar imagery, a land flowing with milk and honey. We will see Jesus agonize in a garden, then resurrect in one. And in the New Heavens and the New Earth, all things will be restored and made gloriously right.

You may be struggling in your relationships right now. Perhaps you're having difficulties in your romantic relationship. This poetry, then, offers hope that someday we will all experience untainted relationships; there will be restoration. And love will be the oxygen of the kingdom.

Lord, thank you for this book that reminds me that marital love can be beautiful, meaningful, and full of hope. Help me to remember the allegories as well, that you are one who deeply loves his people and longs for their wholeness and restoration. Amen.

Day 43

GOD LOVES TRUTH

○ **Morning:** Jeremiah 7–15
○ **Noon:** Jeremiah 16–22
○ **Night:** Psalms 64–65

The prophet Jeremiah, also known as the Weeping Prophet, has much to say to a fledgling Judah. He was part of the Southern Kingdom, living in Judah, and was commissioned by God during the reign of Josiah, a godly king who tore down places of idol worship. However, Josiah's death in battle ended that time of national revival, ushering in an era of apostasy.

Imagine living in a time like that—when up is down and down is up, and you're called by God to try to speak sense into people who hate the truth. No wonder Jeremiah wept!

The Lord's words to this rebellious remnant highlight their desire for lies rather than truth. "Then why do these people stay on their self-destructive path? Why do the people of Jerusalem refuse to turn back? They cling tightly to their lies and will not turn around" (Jeremiah 8:5). When an entire nation clings to lies, destruction tends to follow.

Later in chapter 8, God clarifies even more: "How can you say, 'We are wise because we have the word of the LORD,' when your teachers have twisted it by writing lies? These wise teachers will fall into the trap of their own foolishness, for they have rejected the word of the LORD. Are they so wise after all?" (vv. 8–9).

During this time, so-called prophets were telling Judah that all was well; destruction would not befall them. These were ear-tickling prophecies that kept the people knitted to their lies, making them complacent. The sad thing: When people listen to and believe lies for a long period, as they do here, they begin to believe that lies are truths and truths are lies. In this state, it's difficult to truly determine what is real and what is false.

Jeremiah utters a famous indictment in 17:9, one that we all should heed and memorize. "The human heart is the most deceitful of all things, and desperately wicked. Who really knows how bad it is?" In light of that, what are we to do? This declaration should project us forward into the New Testament, where we finally find a solution to our wicked, deceitful hearts. Only Jesus can take the heart of stone we have and completely transform it.

Jeremiah reminds Judah of this when he highlights what God will do. "But I, the LORD, search all hearts and examine secret motives" (Jeremiah 17:10). When Simeon blessed the new family, Jesus, Mary, and Joseph, he said this about Jesus: "As a result, the deepest thoughts of many hearts will be revealed" (Luke 2:35).

Lord, I want to be so attuned to the truth that I can easily spot a lie. I know how tempting it is to believe lies, particularly because they're often laced with snippets of truth. Please search my heart, make me clean, and give me your perspective on the day ahead. Amen.

Day 44

GOD BLESSES DESPITE EXILE

○ **Morning:** Jeremiah 23–29
○ **Noon:** Jeremiah 30–36
○ **Night:** Psalms 66–67

Today you read one of the most famous Bible verses, Jeremiah 29:11. But did you know that most people rip it from its context to mean something it doesn't mean? To understand it fully, we have to hang out in the preceding chapter, understanding the history of Israel, the nature of the exile, and the promise of the future—something you're currently steeped in.

As you know, the Jewish people disobeyed God in every possible way. They traded him for Baal, preferring to worship demons rather than follow the ways of God. As a direct result of that disobedience, God will send them into Babylonian exile. During that process, we meet Hananiah, a seer. He was one of the so-called prophets mentioned yesterday who prophesied peace, saying they would be returning to Jerusalem soon. His message? All will be well.

Problem was, all would not be well.

Today we see many Hananiahs prophesying the same thing. All will be well. Prosperity is coming. Claim your victory. And then we lump Jeremiah 29:11 in with that—that God knows the plans he has for us, giving us futures and hope. We prefer to believe the Christian life is all about our happiness. We want joy, but we don't want exile to cultivate it. We want holiness without pain.

The context of Jeremiah 29 is exile. Jeremiah chastises Hananiah and prophesies his demise, reminding Judah that their exile would be long. Relief would eventually come, but not swiftly. He encouraged the people to marry and bury, to plant vineyards, to seek the prosperity of their current place.

Jesus said the same thing: "I have told you all this so that you may have peace in me. Here on earth you will have many trials and sorrows. But take heart, because I have overcome the world" (John 16:33). As exiles on this sin-darkened earth, God doesn't tell us to escape our lot, but to find resilience in our exile. Our suffering on earth means something, empowering us to pine for a pristine place.

Yes, of course God knows the plans he has for us. And he will give us a glorious future. But let's remind ourselves that the most profound growth erupts from perseverance, not escapism.

Lord, I want to practice resilience when misfortune or change comes my way. Help me not to try to escape my problems, but to face them with determination and with your strength in me. I want to learn the secret of thriving in exile. Teach me how to have a new heart and new life this year by embracing the exercise of resilience. Amen.

GOD RESCUES FROM CISTERNS

○ **Morning:** Jeremiah 37–44
○ **Noon:** Jeremiah 45–50
○ **Night:** Psalms 68–69

Can you believe it? You are now halfway through this ninety-day Bible reading challenge! May you be making more and more connections in the narrative of the Word of God, and may this exercise utterly change the way you view God, live in his kingdom, and treat others.

In Jeremiah 38, we find the prophet exiled and abandoned in a cistern. King Zedekiah listened to officials who did not like Jeremiah's words about their dire future, so he allowed them to do with Jeremiah as they pleased. "So the officials took Jeremiah from his cell and lowered him by ropes into an empty cistern in the prison yard. It belonged to Malkijah, a member of the royal family. There was no water in the cistern, but there was a thick layer of mud at the bottom, and Jeremiah sank down into it" (Jeremiah 38:6).

A cistern is an empty reservoir that collects water. Because of the nature of drought possibilities, the nation of Israel dug cisterns to capture the rain. When you trace the cistern narrative through the Bible, you'll find some interesting insights. Joseph's cistern experience happened because of his brothers' collective sin.

In Genesis 37:19–24, we see Joseph and his brothers. They decide to throw him into a cistern. Instead of letting him rot there, his brothers sell him to passersby, then promptly lie to their father about his demise and move on with their lives.

Jonah uses pit imagery (similar to cisterns) when he says, "I descended to the roots of the mountains. The earth with its bars was around me forever, But You have brought up my life from the pit, O LORD my God" (Jonah 2:6 NASB). Jonah's pit came about because of his own decision to disobey God.

Jeremiah's cistern sojourn was a result of the sins of others. He did not deserve the descent into mud. God eventually rescued him.

We also see a cistern in the time of Jesus. Between the interrogations by Annas and Caiaphas and the verdict by the Sanhedrin, Jesus was confined, according to Christian tradition, in a dry cistern—typically a pitch-dark hollowed-out hole in limestone. You can visit the place some believe that to be today; it's called the Sacred Pit. So, Jesus knows what it's like to be placed in a pit as a result of someone else's evil choices. He sees you when you're in the cistern, and he knows how to rescue and encourage you.

Lord, I sometimes find myself in a relational pit, where someone has placed me. Help me to turn to you for rescue when that happens. Sometimes, like Jonah, I'm in a pit of my own making. Please convict me when that happens so I can be restored to you. Amen.

Day 46

GOD WILL INTERVENE

○ **Morning:** Jeremiah 51–52
○ **Noon:** Lamentations 1–5
○ **Night:** Psalms 70–71

The book of Lamentations has a very specific poetic structure. The first four chapters are all written in a Hebraic alphabetical acrostic. In other words, if the book were written in English, the first line of each chapter's poem would start with the letter A, and the last line of each chapter's poem would begin with the letter Z. With that in mind, you see the beauty and intricacy of the holy Bible, how intentional and beautiful it is.

The first four chapters are a lament of Jerusalem's fall to Babylon. Chapter 1 looks over the ruins of this once mighty city. The author uses the metaphor of a beautiful royal woman now relegated to slavery. Chapter 2 is another lament of the state of the city, particularly the false prophets and the carnage in the aftermath of such a violent overthrow. Chapter 3 symbolizes a turning point, beginning with grief and ending with a view toward God's ability to rescue his people. Chapter 4 returns to more grief over Jerusalem's devastation.

In chapter 5, we change from lament to petition. This chapter deviates from the acrostic structure; it is simply an all-out prayer by the book's author (thought to be Jeremiah) for God to intervene and usher in salvation.

He begins with a simple statement of truth. "LORD, remember what has happened to us. See how we have been disgraced! Our inheritance has been turned over to strangers, our homes to foreigners" (Lamentations 5:1–2). You can almost hear the pain beneath the writer's words, a cry of hopelessness permeating the besieged city.

He speaks of horrors in the streets, the state of widows and orphans, and the enemy's relentless pursuit. In this plight, there is no rest. He ends his lament with these poignant words: "For Jerusalem is empty and desolate, a place haunted by jackals" (Lamentations 5:18).

This is where the turn happens, and it's instructive. Have you ever felt at the end of your wits, utterly abandoned, and worn out from grief? There is hope—not necessarily in favorable circumstances, but in the faithfulness of the God who loves to intervene. The author shares his turn of attention from destruction to God's goodness: "But LORD, you remain the same forever! Your throne continues from generation to generation" (Lamentations 5:19). He then asks God why he continues to forget them (an honest question), then finishes with hope tinged with the reality of their dire situation.

"Restore us, O LORD, and bring us back to you again! Give us back the joys we once had! Or have you utterly rejected us? Are you angry with us still?" (Lamentations 5:21–22). Life may be difficult, but God remains on his throne and loves to renew our past joy. Rest in that today.

Lord, while I haven't experienced war or this kind of carnage, there are times I feel abandoned and small, helpless to change my circumstances. Thank you that you are faithful even when I'm faithless. Restore me. Please intervene in my life, I pray. Amen.

GOD IS GLORIOUS

○ **Morning:** Ezekiel 1–7
○ **Noon:** Ezekiel 8–15
○ **Night:** Psalms 72–73

The book of Ezekiel begins with glory in the form of a fantastical vision the prophet has about wheels within wheels. It's what's above the vision that causes our hearts to stir. Above everything stood a blue-hued throne with what appeared to be a man atop it. The top part of this "man" glowed, and the bottom part was afire. "All around him was a glowing halo, like a rainbow shining in the clouds on a rainy day. This is what the glory of the LORD looked like to me. When I saw it, I fell face down on the ground, and I heard someone's voice speaking to me" (Ezekiel 1:28).

The glory of God is a dynamic theme throughout the Bible. We see it in creation, as the Spirit hovered over the waters. The Israelites experienced God's glory in the cloud by day and the fire by night. God's glory filled the tabernacle, then the temple.

In today's reading of chapters 8 through 11, we see the devastation that resulted from God's glory leaving their beautiful temple. God would not be with them for a time, but he did promise to restore a remnant and dwell with the nation of Israel once again. All would not be lost. One day God's glory would remain upon the nation of Israel. God's presence would be with them forever.

Later you'll read this promise: "And I will make a covenant of peace with them, an everlasting covenant. . . . I will make my home among them. I will be their God, and they will be my people" (Ezekiel 37:26–27). God, who lives in glory, will once again visit and rest upon the people of Israel.

In the New Testament, Jesus embodied God's glory, becoming a permanent promise of God's presence to the whole world.

Aged Simeon, when he cast his eyes on Jesus, said Jesus was "a light to reveal God to the nations, and . . . the glory of your people Israel" (Luke 2:32). When the dove descended upon Jesus during John the Baptist's baptism of him, it rested upon Jesus and did not leave. He would be carrying that Spirit to his people. The apostle John declared, "We have seen his glory, the glory of the Father's one and only Son" (John 1:14). During the transfiguration, three of the disciples, Peter, James, and John, saw the revealed glory of Jesus.

And now? You behold the glory of God. You are now his temple, and his Spirit rests within you. What a profound, beautiful truth! No matter where you go, you cannot escape the power and glory of God. You'll never be forsaken or abandoned.

Lord, your glory is beautiful. I cannot imagine what it must've been like for Ezekiel to see you upon your throne! And yet, I now carry around in my body your very presence. Help me to never take that truth as pedestrian, but let it be the impetus for me to worship you more! Amen.

✓ Day 48

GOD IS FAITHFUL

○ **Morning:** Ezekiel 16–21
○ **Noon:** Ezekiel 22–27
○ **Night:** Psalms 74–75

While you may be familiar with parables because of the many times Jesus taught using them, we see a lot of parables and stories within Ezekiel's narrative. He is a prophet storyteller. Today we focus on chapter 16, the parable of the unfaithful wife.

In that passage, we see the kindness and compassion of God as well as Israel's utter destitution and need for him. Ezekiel portrays the nation as an unloved, abandoned infant, left in an open field to die under the elements.

And yet, our faithful God was moved by compassion, adopted that abandoned baby girl, and cared for her through to womanhood. He covered her, and he made a covenant with her. He cared for her, surrounding her with nourishment and healthy practices. He adorned her, clothed her in fine linens, and fed her well. She was known far and wide for her exquisite beauty.

In verse fifteen, the word *but* interrupts the reverie. "But you thought your fame and beauty were your own" (Ezekiel 16:15). The Lord says through Ezekiel that the rescued child-turned-woman soon forgot the nurturing of her Father and began to play the prostitute. Not only that, but she also used the splendid things the Father gave her to worship dead idols. She took her jewelry and adorned statues with it, then bowed low in homage to them.

Her debauchery extended to the way she took care of her children, sacrificing them to the gods she had grown to love.

God, of course, is indicting Israel, which had prostituted itself to foreign gods. He diagnoses the depth of Israel's sin in saying, "What a sick heart you have" (Ezekiel 16:30).

The end of the chapter is God explaining why he has given the nation over to the nations—because they have fallen in love with those same nations. It's a just punishment, giving them what they loved.

All is not doom and gloom, however. At the end of this long parable about the rise and demise of Israel, God once again reminds them of his faithfulness. He will establish an everlasting covenant (promise) with the nation. They will repent of their sins. And God, in his utter graciousness, will forgive and restore his people.

This is good news for you too. No matter how far you flee from the presence of God, no matter how you trample upon his covenant, no matter how much your actions resemble the parable of the unfaithful wife, God cannot change his nature. He will always, always be faithful to you.

Lord, thank you for this warning in Ezekiel today. I am so grateful for your faithfulness to a faithless people. And I confess that I am often in that place of faithlessness. Please forgive me for chasing things that are not you, Lord. I choose you instead. And I rest in your forgiveness. Amen.

GOD IS THE GOOD SHEPHERD

○ **Morning:** Ezekiel 28–33
○ **Noon:** Ezekiel 34–39
○ **Night:** Psalms 76–77

Ezekiel 34 is an indictment of the shepherds of the house of Israel, and there are many parallels we're seeing in today's churches. God warns those who supposedly care for the flock that they have lost their way. Instead of feeding their flock, they let them starve. They take care of themselves before genuinely looking after the sheep in their care.

God indicts them for their sins of omission as well. They have not taken care of the wounded in their midst. They have not inconvenienced themselves to bother to look for any straying sheep.

Instead, they have ruled with cruelty. And the result? The scattering of wounded and bleating sheep still in need of a shepherd.

God reminds the evil shepherds that "I now consider these shepherds my enemies, and I will hold them responsible for what has happened to my flock. I will take away their right to feed the flock, and I will stop them from feeding themselves. I will rescue my flock from their mouths; the sheep will no longer be their prey" (Ezekiel 34:10).

Imagine that! The sheep the shepherds were to care for had become their prey. This should not be.

Here's the amazing news. God is the best shepherd we could ever imagine. Even when leaders of his church fail to care for their flock, God promises to care for us. He will search for us, seek us out, and care for us.

Perhaps one of the most beautiful passages in this very long Old Testament book is this one: "I myself will tend my sheep and give them a place to lie down in peace, says the Sovereign LORD. I will search for my lost ones who strayed away, and I will bring them safely home again. I will bandage the injured and strengthen the weak" (Ezekiel 34:15–16).

This passage should also serve as the beacon of a hyperlink toward Jesus Christ, who tells us, "I am the good shepherd. The good shepherd lays down his life for the sheep" (John 10:11 ESV).

When you feel wayward, when other Christians have failed to love and shepherd you, when you sense your lostness, Christ will shepherd you. According to Psalm 23, God will lead you beside quiet waters. He will restore your soul. He will guide you. He will prepare a feast for you even in the presence of your enemies. He loves to guide and help you.

> *Lord, thank you that you are my good shepherd who cares for me well, even when I'm walking astray (particularly then!). In light of what good shepherds do, I pray you'd help me nurture, lead, and tend to those I'm shepherding today. I need your strength. Amen.*

✓ Day 50

GOD REESTABLISHES

○ **Morning:** Ezekiel 40–48
○ **Noon:** Ezra 1–7
○ **Night:** Psalm 78

Today you finish one of the most difficult books of the Bible! Not only that, but today is Day 50! Can you believe you've read the Bible for fifty days? You're more than halfway through, and there is so much to read and experience.

In today's reading, you see Ezekiel's vision for what Israel could be, with a new temple, God's glory, a different allocation of land for the nation, and a healing river that rejuvenates the Dead Sea into a very much alive one. This vision includes trees, fresh water, and crops. "The fruit will be for food and the leaves for healing" (Ezekiel 47:12).

Can you see how this vision echoes the very end of time? In the New Heavens and the New Earth, there is a healing river as well. Note the similarity in language: "It flowed down the center of the main street. On each side of the river grew a tree of life, bearing twelve crops of fruit, with a fresh crop each month. The leaves were used for medicine to heal the nations" (Revelation 22:2).

As you've learned earlier, this is the telescoping nature of prophecy. It is both for the time being and for what is to come, and both can be equally true for two different time periods.

In jumping to Ezra, you see a prophet and a scribe God uses to reestablish Israel after captivity. There are two heroes of this relocation, including today's scribe and tomorrow's official, Nehemiah. Together they establish order, reorient Israel back to covenantal practices, rebuild the wall surrounding Jerusalem, and construct a new iteration of the temple.

Before they can reconstruct the temple, however, the nation must contend with its intermarrying with outsiders. This caused a rift in worship because those married to people who worshiped idols would be tempted to worship God plus non-gods. Ezra dealt decisively with this sin, and the nation repented.

We see two important practices here—the people of God are called to worship God alone, and they are tasked with keeping the nation pure. Holy God, holy people.

Interestingly, when they miraculously completed the new temple, the people both mourned and celebrated—mourned because the new temple paled in comparison to the splendor of Solomon's rendition, and celebrated because they were now established in worship in their land. "The joyful shouting and weeping mingled together in a loud noise that could be heard far in the distance" (Ezra 3:13). Isn't that like life? We learn that pain and joy can coexist.

Lord, thank you for reestablishing the nation of Israel after exile. Like them, I realize there is necessary grief, yet amazing joy. Help me to hold both in tension in my life. And when I'm discouraged, remind me of your life-giving river that is to come. Amen.

GOD WORKS THROUGH REMNANTS

○ **Morning:** Ezra 8–10
○ **Noon:** Nehemiah 1–9
○ **Night:** Psalms 79–80

Nehemiah, under the blessing of the Persian king Artaxerxes, returns to a ruined Jerusalem, intent on rebuilding the once-powerful wall around it. His is an impossible and monumental task.

Many leadership gurus have studied the way Nehemiah motivated the nation to rebuild, and there are several important principles to glean from his ingenuity. First, as the title of today's entry indicates, he knew that God used those who remained, the remnants. Nehemiah couldn't conjure up a different workforce. He had returned exiles as well as some of those left behind to do this mighty work. What an encouragement that God doesn't use the capable and strong as much as he uses the outcasts and broken to do his best work!

Nehemiah also believed in the power of prayer. He prayed through the construction process, knowing that this was God's task, not his.

He understood the concept of buy-in: Each family was responsible for erecting the portion of the wall next to their dwelling.

The cupbearer also faced intense persecution and pushback. He certainly had enemies who sought to undermine him and his work. So, he charged half the people to stand guard while the other half built the wall. He understood the people's fear of attack.

I love what he retorted to his enemies trying to distract him: "I am engaged in a great work, so I can't come. Why should I stop working to come and meet with you?" (Nehemiah 6:3). He is an example for all of us. Instead of letting the naysayers discourage us, we must simply continue our work in God's kingdom.

Nehemiah took care of the broken, particularly those bent beneath the load of debt. He told those charging interest to cease charging it. He knew that the well-being of those building the wall would be undermined by hunger or worry.

Miraculously, the ragtag bunch of remnants completed the wall in fifty-two days. This is a reminder that God can do anything. His power is made alive through the small.

Lord, thank you for the example of Nehemiah, who prayed, was wise, fought spiritual battles, and took care of his people. Help me hide these lessons of bravery in my heart for the week ahead. I often feel like a remnant, but I'm so grateful you empower remnants to do great things in your kingdom. Amen.

GOD DELIVERS THROUGH THE UNLIKELY

○ **Morning:** Nehemiah 10–13
○ **Noon:** Esther 1–10
○ **Night:** Psalms 81–83

Though some have argued to omit the book of Esther from the canon of Scripture (God is not mentioned, for example), the story remains an important reminder of God's ability to take care of his people.

Esther, an orphan raised by her cousin Mordecai, finds herself in a precarious position—elevated to be queen to a pagan king, Xerxes, who has fickly placed his first queen, Vashti, in exile. Amidst all this is an evil plotter, Haman, who wants to annihilate all the Jews because Mordecai will not bow down to him.

This book is the impetus for the festival of Purim that Jewish people still commemorate today by exchanging gifts of food and drink, donating to the poor, and eating a celebratory meal together. Jewish people read the book of Esther in its entirety after fasting first (as Esther did). When Haman is named, people boo him! When Mordecai is mentioned, cheers erupt. This festival is the only celebration of common Jewish practice today that was not initiated by Moses.

Included in this book is a lesson for us today about the end game of racial prejudice. Taken to its extreme, mass murder is acceptable to those who hate one group of people. Sadly, we have seen this kind of ethnic cleansing take place throughout history and certainly in today's world.

God often uses deliverers who don't fit the mold of a superhero. Moses murdered a man and stuttered. Rahab was a prostitute.

David was the last born of his family and nearly forgotten. And Esther? She was a woman essentially trafficked into her position, who faced death by even daring to enter the king's presence without being invited. Not only that, but she had no living lineage other than her cousin Mordecai to establish her.

Even so, Esther did two powerful things we can learn from. She told the truth about the untenable decree against her people. And she resisted that evil by taking a huge personal risk. In looking back on Nazi Germany and the holocaust, it is the truth-telling resisters we laud as heroic. To combat the evil of genocide, action is required; passivity allows it.

It's never easy to tell the truth when lies are the popular language of our time. Nor is it easy to stand up for those who cannot speak for themselves. Both involve heroic risk and a strong reliance on the God who uses ordinary people like us to bring deliverance for many.

Lord, wow. I'm impressed by both Esther and Mordecai, by their love for their people and their fearless choices to protect them. Help me to be a truth teller and a protector like that. I want to remember this lesson for the rest of my life. Amen.

GOD IS IN THE FIRE

○ **Morning:** Daniel 1–6
○ **Noon:** Daniel 7–12
○ **Night:** Psalms 84–85

In today's reading, we are unpacking the exile and the return from exile. So, we're backing up a bit by reading Daniel, though we just read about the return to Jerusalem and the rebuilding of the walls and the temple in Ezra and Nehemiah.

Daniel is a faithful follower of God. He is wise, measured, disciplined, and (eventually) prophetic, which is why he is one of the major prophets.

Babylon became Daniel's home during the exile, having hailed from a royal family in Judah before the conquest. He treated King Nebuchadnezzar with respect and earned a good reputation in exile. He did not indulge in the rich foods of the king's fare, relegating himself to eating vegetables and water. You may have heard of people following a "Daniel fast." That practice came from Daniel's habit highlighted in chapter 1.

Daniel ingratiates himself to the king by interpreting a dream, but then Daniel's friends infuriate his royal highness by *not* bowing down to the king's golden statue. This is where we find the famous Sunday School story of the fiery furnace.

The fire was so intense that it killed the soldiers who threw the three men into the furnace. And yet? They were not even singed—and in the middle of the raging fire, another man stood in their midst. "'Look!' Nebuchadnezzar shouted, 'I see four men, unbound, walking around in the fire unharmed! And the fourth looks like a god!'" (Daniel 3:25). This sighting could be what scholars call a *theophany*, a visual encounter with God himself.

You may remember a verse tucked into the narrative of Isaiah that promises, "When you go through deep waters, I will be with you. When you go through rivers of difficulty, you will not drown. When you walk through the fire of oppression, you will not be burned up; the flames will not consume you" (Isaiah 43:2). These three men certainly were being oppressed because of their belief in God, and yet they were not burned up or consumed.

The powerful point of this story is not that they didn't burn up. The three acknowledged that God, in his sovereignty, could choose *not* to rescue them. Instead, the lesson is that God's presence was with them in the adversity—a promise he gives to you today as well.

And not only that, but the pagan king turned from his ways and began to praise the God of Israel because of this miracle. So, stay the course. Walk with integrity. Trust in God. Experience him in the pain. And who knows? Maybe a Nebuchadnezzar in your life will end up praising God!

Lord, what an example of faith in you. Help me to trust you through my own fiery trials today. Thank you that you will never, ever leave me. Thank you that you see me. Thank you that you do the miraculous. I lift up the Nebuchadnezzar in my life and pray for their salvation. Amen.

✓ Day 54

GOD LONGS FOR OUR RETURN

○ **Morning:** Haggai 1–2
○ **Noon:** Zechariah 1–14
○ **Night:** Psalms 86–88

I hope you're hearing the heartbeat of God as you read each day. You may have heard or thought that God seemed mean in the Old Testament and kindhearted in the New, but in actuality, God is constantly beckoning his people to himself. He longs for their fellowship. He wants them to return to him, wholeheartedly. His desire is to be close with his creation.

In Zechariah 1:3, we hear these echoes of God's compassion: "Therefore, say to the people, 'This is what the LORD of Heaven's Armies says: Return to me, and I will return to you, says the LORD of Heaven's Armies.'"

Zechariah's prophecies throughout this minor prophet's book hint at this return and restoration—that once again God would dwell alongside his people. "People will come from distant lands to rebuild the Temple of the LORD. And when this happens, you will know that my messages have been from the LORD of Heaven's Armies. All this will happen if you carefully obey what the LORD your God says" (Zechariah 6:15).

God's presence dwells with those who dare to return, to those who obey his voice. But even in this requirement, God provides people (including you and me) with the means and ability to repent. One of Zechariah's famous sayings reminds us, "This is what the LORD says to Zerubbabel: It is not by force nor by strength, but by my Spirit, says the LORD of Heaven's Armies" (Zechariah 4:6).

In our own strength, we cannot usher in God's presence. In our power, it is difficult to turn away from sin and turn toward the Lord. Jesus reminds us of this truth when he says, "For no one can come to me unless the Father who sent me draws them to me, and at the last day I will raise them up" (John 6:44).

God promises to draw us, be with us, and lift us up. The minor prophet Haggai reminds us, "My Spirit remains among you, just as I promised when you came out of Egypt. So do not be afraid" (Haggai 2:5). When we return to God, we remember his ever-present Spirit, and in that remembrance, our fears have a chance to dissipate.

> *Lord, I want to return to you. Please draw me to yourself. I realize I need you even when I'm trying to repent. Thank you that your Spirit is with me wherever I go. I am never alone. I am never forsaken or lost. Thank you for loving me that much. Amen.*

Day 55

GOD REIGNS OVER HISTORY

○ **Morning:** Malachi 1–4
○ **Noon:** 1 Chronicles 1–14
○ **Night:** Psalm 89

You may be experiencing a little historical whiplash today. Malachi brings us to the brink of the intertestamental period, the quiet part of history between Israel's return from exile and the time of Jesus.

But then we jumped backward to the book of Chronicles. The name of the book gives you a strong clue about its contents. It's a chronicle of the history of Israel, penned by a chronicler. Traditionally, the author of this book is Ezra the scribe—a historian. He divides his work in two pieces—revealing the history of Israel through many genealogies (even through the exile), then backing up to detail the rise of King David, then the building of the temple by Solomon.

While it can be tedious to read genealogies, what stands out is the importance of individuals and their communities. Their names matter. Where people lived points to the story of Israel. God takes care of all of them, preserving a line throughout generations of people who strayed, obeyed, or lived in indifference to God.

We see the intervention of God tucked in these genealogies. In one case, "They cried out to God during the battle, and he answered their prayer because they trusted in him. So the Hagrites and all their allies were defeated" (1 Chronicles 5:20). God hears the cries of those who are oppressed and rescues them from disaster.

We also see the uniqueness of individuals chronicled here: "He had a daughter named Sheerah. She built the towns of Lower and Upper Beth-horon and Uzzen-sheerah" (1 Chronicles 7:24). What an industrious woman! How beautiful that she is forever memorialized in Scripture for her hard work and creativity.

We end today's reading with David coming on the scene, a pivotal point of Israel's history. He brings worship to Jerusalem, experiences the holiness of God when Uzzah touches the ark of the covenant (and dies), and then defeats the Philistines. We close our history lesson with these powerful words: "So David's fame spread everywhere, and the LORD caused all the nations to fear David" (1 Chronicles 14:17).

You can almost hear the dun-dun-dun of a historical pivot because we know that David's intermarriage, his assault of Bathsheba and killing of her husband, and the downfall of his kingdom will be imminent. And with Solomon's many, many wives, we will see the turning of the heart of the king of Israel away from God and toward pagan worship. Think of Chronicles as a condensed version of the history of the nation, but remind yourself that, even so, God rules and reigns over his people.

> *Lord, sometimes I just need to read history to remind myself that you are on the throne, and all will be well. Thank you for reigning even when the world spins into worry and stress. Thank you that you are unfazed by historical events, but you hold them all in your hands. Amen.*

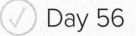 Day 56

GOD PROMISES AN EVERLASTING KINGDOM

○ **Morning:** 1 Chronicles 15–21
○ **Noon:** 1 Chronicles 22–29
○ **Night:** Psalms 90–91

David's advice to his son Solomon are words meant to encourage us as well. He says, "Be strong and courageous, and do the work. Don't be afraid or discouraged, for the LORD God, my God, is with you. He will not fail you or forsake you. He will see to it that all the work related to the Temple of the LORD is finished correctly" (1 Chronicles 28:20).

Do you hear echoes of Joshua's words here? He uttered these to the nation of Israel prior to their conquest of the Promised Land, and now we hear the same call to action as the nation establishes itself by a temple. No longer will they wander and conquer. Now they will bravely settle and worship.

The Lord spoke over David, encouraging him, and establishing his dynasty forever. This kingdom of David's will not be temporal, but everlasting. The Lord said through the prophet Nathan, "For when you die and join your ancestors, I will raise up one of your descendants, one of your sons, and I will make his kingdom strong" (1 Chronicles 17:11).

David understood this surprising provision when he prayed a prayer of thanks, saying, "And now, it has pleased you to bless the house of your servant, so that it will continue forever before you. For when you grant a blessing, O LORD, it is an eternal blessing!" (1 Chronicles 17:27).

The one who chronicled the events of the house of David, then the rise and fall of Solomon, must have been surprised by exile. It seemed the promises of God were thwarted. He could not see what we have the privilege of seeing now: Jesus, in the lineage of David, would usher in an entirely different kingdom. This is why when Jesus walked the earth, he constantly taught about the kingdom of God.

Jesus's dynasty is an eternal one. He is King over all creation, not merely a nation. He is royalty reigning over the church as a husband loves his wife. He sacrificed his life, willingly laying it down for his subjects (us!). Jesus was the King Israel needed but didn't expect. He didn't usher in a period of political peace. Instead, this Prince of Peace brought about peace between sinful humankind and a holy God.

King Jesus sits on a throne at the right hand of the Father, ever interceding for his subjects, us. He cannot die. He rules forever. And someday, he will return and take us home. This is the Good News of the kingdom of God.

Lord, thank you for showing me how you fulfilled the idea of an everlasting kingdom through the line of David. Thank you that you are now the ruler of a never-ending realm, and that I have the audacious privilege of being your child. Amen.

GOD DWELLS IN A TEMPLE

○ **Morning:** 2 Chronicles 1–9
○ **Noon:** 2 Chronicles 10–17
○ **Night:** Psalms 92–94

God's name is on the temple of God that Solomon created. Today you read a beautiful prayer of dedication for that glorious, shining temple, uttered by Solomon in 2 Chronicles 6. He addresses God as faithful, holy, and a promise keeper. He rightfully takes a position of humility when he says, "But will God really live on earth among people? Why, even the highest heavens cannot contain you. How much less this Temple I have built!" (2 Chronicles 6:18).

He continues, "May you watch over this Temple day and night, this place where you have said you would put your name. May you always hear the prayers I make toward this place" (2 Chronicles 6:20). That God's name rests on the temple is significant. It means God's presence, power, and availability reside there. When God's name is associated with a place, it means it is his alone—he owns it.

Interestingly, Solomon uses God's personal name when he prays—the hushed *Yahweh*. This temple would be the center of the nation's worship. It would be a physical symbol of God's covenant with his chosen people. This beautiful name of God would be revered, worshiped, and honored in this place.

We can't help but look forward to another temple in the day of Jesus, where he turned over tables, confronted religious leaders, and performed many miracles. He equated himself with the temple when he said, "All right. . . . Destroy this temple, and in three days I will raise it up" (John 2:19).

Later, post-resurrection in the dawn of the church, Peter reveals the new temple of God when he urges people to come "to Christ, who is the living cornerstone of God's temple. He was rejected by people, but he was chosen by God for great honor. And you are living stones that God is building into his spiritual temple. What's more, you are his holy priests. Through the mediation of Jesus Christ, you offer spiritual sacrifices that please God" (1 Peter 2:4–5).

So, we see God dwelling with his people through a cloud, fire, the tabernacle, the temple, through Jesus, and now in his glorious church. We can clearly see that God's intention all along was to be with his people, right next to them, and now within them.

What a privilege to be the container of the presence of God, to be his dwelling place today. What joy to never be left alone, to carry with us the very nature and companionship of the God of the universe!

> *Lord, thank you that I am now your temple, that you dwell in me. I pray I never get over the amazingness of your presence with me wherever I go. Thank you for teaching me the history of your presence. I'm grateful for you. Amen.*

GOD ENCOURAGES STRONG FINISHERS

○ **Morning:** 2 Chronicles 18–24
○ **Noon:** 2 Chronicles 25–31
○ **Night:** Psalms 95–96

It's important to take note of faithful leaders, kings, and prophets in the Old Testament because of their rarity. So often, peppered in Israel's narrative, leaders behave badly, chasing after idols and rejecting God.

But not Uzziah. He's the son of King Amaziah, who died when Uzziah was just sixteen years old, and he ruled for over five decades. He was king of Judah in the southern part of the divided kingdom. He decisively dealt with the Philistines and built a plethora of cities. It's even said in the text that he became very powerful, enough to impress the Egyptians. He armed his regiments well, and he prevailed against his enemies.

But then something happened in Uzziah's heart. He forsook the advice from long ago (Deuteronomy 8:14, 17) that warned, "Do not become proud at that time and forget the LORD your God, who rescued you from slavery in the land of Egypt. . . . He did all this so you would never say to yourself, 'I have achieved this wealth with my own strength and energy.'" Uzziah forsook the wisdom of Proverbs 16:18, "Pride goes before destruction, and haughtiness before a fall."

The Scripture says, "But when he had become powerful, he also became proud, which led to his downfall" (2 Chronicles 26:16). You read today how he tried to act like a priest, entering the temple—even after eighty priests and the high priest chased after him and warned him not to do such a blasphemous thing. In his pride, he disregarded their wisdom.

Uzziah began well, probably with good intentions for the nation he ruled. But the sinister temptress of pride captured his heart, then his actions. He did not finish well. Instead of ruling like a great king, he was relegated to a separate house because the Lord struck him with leprosy while he burned incense like a priest. He died with leprosy, having lived the latter part of his reign in isolation.

And yet, there is always hope. In the year he died, God raised up Isaiah, the great prophet to the nation, whose prophecy would help navigate the pain of exile.

This is an important lesson for us all. Many people can begin their ministries or jobs or roles well, with youthful vigor and good intention. But it is rare for someone to live faithfully over the long haul, what Eugene Peterson termed, in the title of his book on discipleship, *A Long Obedience in the Same Direction*. To finish well is to persevere, not give up, and live with humility. When we do so, we receive grace. "God opposes the proud but gives grace to the humble" (James 4:6).

Lord, I want to finish my race here on earth with intention and humility. Help me remember the pride of Uzziah when I'm tempted to give into my self-centeredness and self-importance. Thank you for sharing cautionary tales with me in your Word. Amen.

GOD SENDS JESUS!

○ **Morning:** 2 Chronicles 32–36
○ **Noon:** Matthew 1–4
○ **Night:** Psalms 97–99

You have made it through the entire Old Testament (apart from a few psalms). Shout your conquest from the rooftops! What an accomplishment! According to a 2016 Lifeway study, you're nearing the 20 percent of Americans who have read the whole Bible. More than 50 percent said they've read little or none of it.[1] I pray this adventure has opened your eyes to the beauty of the Old Testament, that you're seeing connections you've never uncovered before, and that you're falling in love with God's powerful Word.

Today we meet the hero of our story—Jesus the Christ. He has come to reverse the effects of the fall, deal decisively with humankind's sinful nature, and reveal his power not only over sin, but also over death.

You may be reading the genealogy of Jesus with new eyes, now that you just finished the Old Testament. Matthew traces Jesus from Abraham to his earthly father, Joseph, with notable nods to Ruth, David, Bathsheba, Solomon, Uzziah (whom we read about yesterday), Josiah, and Zerubbabel, who rebuilt the temple. His lineage consists of people within and without the nation of Israel, and it includes David to show us that he is a son of David—which points to his messianic possibility.

In these short chapters, you see the miraculous birth of Jesus; the preparation of John the Baptist, who acts as almost a second Elijah, preparing the way for the Messiah; the baptism of Jesus when the presence of God remained upon him; and the temptation of Jesus immediately after God's declaration that Jesus is his son.

The temptation of Jesus has been dissected and written about by many scholars over the course of history, but for today, take note of how often Jesus looks backward to the Old Testament as part of his arsenal against the devil. It's interesting to note that Jesus stays in the Pentateuch in rebuking the devil with Scripture, particularly the book of Deuteronomy.

Whereas the nation of Israel complained about bread in the wilderness, Jesus resisted the temptation of hunger to feed instead on the goodness of God. While the nation of Israel put God to the test (often), Jesus chose not to. Where Israel longed for political prowess and would have jumped at the opportunity to become the most powerful nation on earth, Jesus shrugged that opportunity off, preferring to trust his Father for his timing and his ways (which would not look like political overthrow).

In reading this temptation story, we realize someone better than Israel has come onto the scene, able to walk through the wilderness with his integrity and heart intact.

Lord, thank you for sustaining me through the reading of the Old Testament. Thank you for how your Word is woven together in a stunning tapestry of your redemption. Thank you for sending Jesus into this world so that I could be rescued from my sin. Amen.

Day 60

GOD WRITES A PERFECT SERMON

○ **Morning:** Matthew 5–8
○ **Noon:** Matthew 9–12
○ **Night:** Psalms 100–102

Today you read the entire Sermon on the Mount, Jesus's famous words about how this new kingdom would look. It would not be a political realm, but it would manifest itself as a people who act in love.

What's powerful about this sermon is how it points to Jesus as being greater than Moses. Note their similarities: Moses came out of Egypt; Jesus's family was exiled to Egypt to preserve his life, then returned to Judea. Moses passed through the Red Sea prior to forty years in the wilderness; Jesus passed through the waters of baptism in the Jordan river right before he entered the wilderness of temptation for forty days. Moses received the law on Mount Sinai, then delivered it to the people; Jesus received the law from his Father in heaven (on high), then delivered it to the people as he taught from a mountain.

Moses represented the Old Covenant, based on God's faithfulness and humankind's fidelity to God's law. Jesus inaugurated the New Covenant, based entirely on his finished work on the cross followed by his resurrection.

All this is cause for celebration. Someone more authoritative than Moses stood before the people proclaiming favor and blessing upon them. Have you ever wondered where the word *beatitude* came from? The Latin Vulgate translated *blessed* (in Greek) to *beati*, therefore all these "blessed" sayings are called the Beatitudes as a result.

The Greek word for blessed here is *makarios*. It means to extend or enhance one's state of blessedness. So, when you're poor or mourning or persecuted, God's mercy and kindness toward you are enlarged. The Amplified Bible (Classic Edition) translates *blessed* in Matthew 5:3 this way: "happy, to be envied, and spiritually prosperous—with life-joy and satisfaction in God's favor and salvation, regardless of their outward conditions." What a beautiful mouthful!

Of note is that Jesus doesn't conform to the typical concept of Jewish blessing from the Old Testament. There, if you are faithful and do everything right, you will be materially blessed. But here, Jesus flips the script. When you are in a deep state of need, that's when you realize your need for God. In that need, you search for him, then receive him in abundance. In other words, things can never fill you, but your need will be filled by the presence of God. And in that state, you are truly blessed.

That's why we can rejoice in our sufferings because in those sufferings, our needs are exposed more clearly, and we can't help but reach for help. The Gospel is about a holy God reaching for humankind as we stretch our arms toward him. He loves us enough to rescue us during our pain journey, providing the strength we need to endure it, and to find blessing as we walk as children in the new kingdom. Even when we mourn, we are blessed. Even when we face persecution, God brings blessing. This is good news, indeed.

Lord, thank you for your sermon about blessing. I'm so grateful that I can experience your presence and help when I walk through various trials and worries. Thank you for being greater than Moses, and for how the Scriptures reveal such harmony. Amen.

✓ Day 61

GOD PROVIDES A SURPRISING MESSIAH

- ○ **Morning:** Matthew 13–16
- ○ **Noon:** Matthew 17–20
- ○ **Night:** Psalm 103

Congratulations! Today you've covered two-thirds of the Bible, and you have only one-third to go! What a significant accomplishment!

Today's passage includes a noted conversation in which Jesus asks his disciples who people think he is. Most people see him as a prophet like John the Baptist returned from the dead, or Elijah, or Jeremiah. But Peter utters what must have been shocking to his Jewish friends. "You are the Messiah, the Son of the living God" (Matthew 16:16).

The Jewish term for messiah is *mashiakh*, which means anointed one. The Greek word you may recognize as *christos*.

Most Jewish people saw the coming Messiah as a heroic war victor. You hear echoes of that in Zechariah 9:9–10.

> Rejoice, O people of Zion!
>   Shout in triumph, O people of Jerusalem!
> Look, your king is coming to you.
>   He is righteous and victorious,
> yet he is humble, riding on a donkey—
>   riding on a donkey's colt.
> I will remove the battle chariots from Israel
>   and the warhorses from Jerusalem.
> I will destroy all the weapons used in battle,
>   and your king will bring peace to the nations.
> His realm will stretch from sea to sea
>   and from the Euphrates River to the ends of the earth.

Note how the prophet's words accurately predict Jesus's triumphal entry, but also speak of victory and peace and a fortified, robust nation.

Jesus's life and the way he lived it pointed the nation of Israel back to Isaiah's difficult predictions of the Suffering Servant. "He was despised and rejected—a man of sorrows, acquainted with deepest grief. We turned our backs on him and looked the other way. He was despised, and we did not care. . . . He was oppressed and treated harshly, yet he never said a word. He was led like a lamb to the slaughter. And as a sheep is silent before the shearers, he did not open his mouth" (Isaiah 53:3, 7).

It's startling to read Isaiah's words and see just how perfectly Jesus fit them. But even though predicted otherwise, Israel could not deviate in their thinking that the messiah would be a victorious Rome-abolisher, freeing them from governmental oppression and establishing their kingdom as superior.

Jesus, to their surprise, was building an entirely different kingdom, where those who followed him would be set free, not from governments, but from the powers of hell. He would not be a messiah for one nation and one political situation, but the Christ who delivered the entire world from the grip of sin and death.

Lord, thank you for being the kind of messiah who chased the whole world, including me. I'm so grateful yours was not a geopolitical victory, but a victory over the powers of darkness. You were not what many expected, but you were who everyone needed. Amen.

GOD SENDS US

○ **Morning:** Matthew 21–24
○ **Noon:** Matthew 25–28
○ **Night:** Psalm 104

So much happens in the last chapter of Matthew. Jesus appears to two Marys—blessedly alive. They're tasked with telling the disciples about his resurrection. The leading priests bribed the men guarding the tomb to say people stole Jesus's body. On a mountain out of earshot of the crowds, Jesus gathers his eleven remaining disciples and gives what is commonly known as the Great Commission.

A scattered, ragtag bunch of disciples, once cowering and flee-ing, is now tasked with taking the message of Jesus to the whole known world. How can this possibly happen?

Jesus begins by reminding them of his authority. As Creator, he has all (not some) control over the domain of creation. As God in the flesh, he is ruler over heaven as well. Because of this, he has the right to grant the disciples the ability and stamina to proclaim him everywhere.

He is not a dead messiah, amounting to nothing. He is not a blip of history, soon forgotten. No, he is unique and powerful, able to rise from the dead. He is supreme over all, precisely because of the resurrection.

Because of that, Jesus commands them (and us!) to go to the nations, the very heartbeat of God from the beginning. Israel, as you've been uncovering, was meant to be a city on a hill, a beacon for all nations to finally come to the One who created them. Post-resurrection, the invitation is not merely for the Jewish people, but for all people—everywhere.

Jesus tasks all his disciples not only with proclaiming his life, death, and resurrection, but to also perform baptism—an outward sign of an inward decision. That baptism is weighted with the Trinity. We are to baptize in the name of the Father, the Son, and the Holy Spirit.

Not only that, we are not tasked merely with proclaiming and baptizing, but with discipling the nations. Those who meet Jesus for the first time and acknowledge him through baptism also need to learn what it means to follow him day in and day out. To disciple others is to simply walk alongside them, doing life together, breaking bread, praying, and encouraging. It's a journey of listening, caring, and telling the truth in love.

Such a grand task!

But thankfully, Jesus finishes his commissioning by reminding the disciples that he will never, ever leave them. He will be with them as they disciple the world.

> Lord, I feel small as I consider your Great Commission. Help me to share you with others this week. Teach me what it means to disciple the people in my life. I also pray you'd send someone to help me learn how to be a more faithful disciple. Amen.

GOD LOOKS INSIDE

○ **Morning:** Mark 1–4
○ **Noon:** Mark 5–8
○ **Night:** Psalm 105

The Jewish leaders were stressed.

In chapter 7, we read that "they noticed that some of his [Jesus's] disciples failed to follow the Jewish ritual of hand washing before eating" (Mark 7:2). They asked Jesus why in the world his followers didn't properly follow tradition.

Jesus confounds them with his answer, as he often does. One interesting study you can do of the gospels (after this rapid read) is to take note of when Jesus confused, confounded, or bothered people, particularly when he defied expectations. You'll find he constantly does this.

In Mark 7:6–7, Jesus quotes Isaiah 29:13, a passage the Jewish leaders would have been familiar with: "'These people honor me with their lips, but their hearts are far from me. Their worship is a farce, for they teach man-made ideas as commands from God.'" Thus begins his pointed discourse about the religious leaders' penchant for missing the entire point. God is not after external rituals that are meant to impress others with their piety. He always, always looks internally to the heart.

It's not what we put into our bodies or the way we do so that matters. It's what is in our hearts that reveals where we are with the Lord. "It's not what goes into your body that defiles you; you are defiled by what comes from your heart" (Mark 7:15). Later, he clarifies: "For from within, out of a person's heart, come evil thoughts, sexual immorality, theft, murder, adultery, greed, wickedness, deceit, lustful desires, envy, slander, pride, and foolishness"

(Mark 7:21–22). That's a disturbing list, and it must have shocked the wash-your-hands-before-you-eat legalism of the religious elite.

Interestingly, after this encounter, Jesus moved on to minister to a Gentile woman, someone considered utterly unclean by the Jewish people. Even though she knew it was culturally inappropriate for her to approach Jesus, she did so anyway. Her heart for her demon-oppressed daughter overcame her propriety.

They have an interesting interaction in which it appears Jesus is being mean by referring to her in the same manner many Jews would—as a dog. Remember, Jesus always has an audience, and he is using this interaction as a teaching moment for his disciples. He already knows the woman's response because he knows her heart. When she responds in beautiful faith, Jesus heals her daughter from afar.

In these two stories, you see irony. The religious leaders who are supposedly clean have dirty hearts. The Gentile woman who is supposedly dirty has a clean, faith-filled heart. Jesus is more interested in the inside of us than he is in religious performance.

Lord, thank you for reminding me today that how I appear on the outside is not what you care about. You look to the heart. Would you search my heart and help me to wholeheartedly follow you? I do love you, and I long for my heart to be pure. Amen.

GOD BECKONS US TO FOLLOW

○ **Morning:** Mark 9–11
○ **Noon:** Mark 12–16
○ **Night:** Psalm 106

One of the most common words in the New Testament is *peripateo*, which simply means to walk alongside or to travel along. Throughout the gospels you see Jesus walking to and from places and his disciples following him around. This was not an easy adventure. Having been to Israel, I realize just how much walking they experienced, up and down steep hills, particularly on difficult paths that the disciples trod.

But Jesus's call to the disciples was not to simply walk places with him. He wanted them to follow him wherever he led. He knew he would not always be with them. He knew his mission was to be a sacrificial lamb for the world, followed by a mind-bending resurrection. Jesus would not leave his disciples alone, but he would grant them the Holy Spirit, a constant walking companion.

The church would dawn as the disciples chose to follow Jesus wherever he led. So, when he walked the earth, he trained them to do so. To follow meant leaving everything else behind—even parents, places, or possessions. When he met with the rich young ruler, this latter part was tested. Jesus tells him he can certainly follow him, but first sell everything.

Following Jesus appealed to the man until he heard Jesus's pointed words. Money's hold on him was far greater than his desire to follow Jesus. We know from other passages in the Gospels that you cannot serve both God and money.

It may seem impossible to be able to follow Jesus wherever he leads, but Jesus promises to help those who struggle. "Humanly speaking, it is impossible. But not with God. Everything is possible with God" (Mark 10:27). Jesus provides the strength we need to follow him, particularly in the person of the Holy Spirit dwelling within us.

Not only does he empower us to follow him, but there are also blessings when we do so. He promises us entrance into his amazing kingdom. Forgiveness is ours for the asking. He has adopted us into his family, the church. We will live in delight in the New Heavens and the New Earth where every tear will be wiped away, every sorrow accounted for and salved.

To follow Jesus is to partake on a walking adventure that brings healing, wholeness, freedom, and abundant life. Yes, we give up everything to follow him, but we gain everything in return.

Lord, I want to follow you. I want to walk with you, know you, hear your voice, and experience your presence every day of my life. Show me what I am clinging to instead of following you. Help me forsake those things that hold me back so I can fully chase after you. Amen.

GOD PROVIDES SIGNS

○ **Morning:** John 1–4
○ **Noon:** John 5–8
○ **Night:** Psalm 107

In the Synoptic Gospels (Matthew, Mark, Luke), the authors use the Greek word *dunamis* to describe the miracles Jesus does. You may see the word dynamite in that word, and you'd be correct. *Dunamis* means power. When people experienced miracles in those gospels, they were overwhelmed with awe at the power of God at work.

However, when you read John's gospel, a shift occurs. He doesn't use the same word to describe Jesus's miracles. Instead, he uses *semeion,* a Greek word that simply means "sign," as well as *erga,* which means "works." Later in the high-priestly prayer, Jesus prays, "I brought glory to you here on earth by completing the work you gave me to do" (John 17:4). These signs and works were meant to show the Jewish people that Jesus truly was who he said he was.

When you read through the book of John, you'll see eight miracles recorded: turning water in wine, restoring an official's son, helping a paralyzed man to his feet, providing food for 5,000 hungry people (and then some!), walking on water, restoring sight to a blind man, raising Lazarus from the dead (wow!), and helping bring in a miraculous catch of fish, post-resurrection.

In each instance, belief follows the sign, which was the point.

Each work revealed something about Jesus the Messiah. He could control the elements of nature. He could fix the human body, from brokenness to wholeness. He could rebuild tissue. He could create provision from nothing. He could defy the laws of physics.

He could rewire a human brain. He could overcome death. He could command fish to jump into nets.

So, we are all faced with what we do with these signs. These works of Jesus are meant to be proof of his divinity. And since only the Creator of the universe could do such work, how now shall we live?

As we learned yesterday, Jesus simply asks us to follow him, to be faithful to him, to obey him. Because he is King of kings and Lord of lords, as his followers, we should revere him as such. He deserves our worship, our allegiance, our lives.

These signs are not everyday occurrences, nor are they pedestrian. They are specifically meant to awe us, to hush us, to cause us to ponder. Jesus is unlike any other human being to walk this earth. Not only that, but in the hypostatic union of 100 percent man and 100 percent God, he is mystery. Jesus proved he was the Son of God, then obeyed his Father by willingly offering his life for us on the cross. He ultimately defied death, offering us life.

Lord, thank you, thank you, thank you for your life, obedience, and works. They remind me that you are the Lord of all creation, and you deserve my worship. I am in awe of who you are. Thank you for providing signs for me to see who you really are. Thank you for dying for me. Amen.

GOD ADVOCATES FOR US

○ **Morning:** John 9–13
○ **Noon:** John 14–18
○ **Night:** Psalms 108–109

In John chapters 14 through 16, we learn about the Holy Spirit that Jesus is going to give his disciples. Because the Holy Spirit descended upon Jesus and remained on him, Jesus could say, "But you know him, because he lives with you now and later will be in you" (John 14:17). The word Jesus referred to when he mentioned the promised Holy Spirit is *parakletos,* which means an advocate, much like the lawyer who advocates for someone on trial. That lawyer is always on the side of the defendant and does everything he or she can to help the accused.

It's important to note that Jesus says he will give the disciples *another* advocate (see John 14:16). This means that Jesus was an advocate when he walked alongside the disciples, but that he would be giving a different advocate after his death and resurrection. Imagine how confused the disciples would be hearing this news! What could it mean?

Jesus shares five ways the Spirit would help the disciples, and they mirror the work Jesus did on this earth.

The first is this idea of advocacy—the Spirit would operate as a counselor advocate when the disciples needed help and direction.

The second comes from John 14:26: "But when the Father sends the Advocate as my representative—that is, the Holy Spirit—he will teach you everything and will remind you of everything I have told you." The Spirit helps us remember God's Word and words.

The third we find in John 15:26, where Jesus refers to the Advocate as "the Spirit of truth." The Spirit helps us discern truth from error.

The fourth aspect of the Spirit's help we find in John 16:8, and it's more global. The very Spirit within the disciples will help convict the world of sin and make the world aware of a coming judgment.

The fifth way the Spirit will help the disciples is found in John 16:12–15. Not only will the Spirit help the disciples discern truth from error, but he will disclose to them the very thoughts of Jesus! There's a predictive nature of this, empowering the disciples to get a glimpse of what may come.

What an amazing gift, the Spirit. He is our defense attorney, teacher, truth-teller, convicting one (for the world), and our personal discloser. Because these promises are extended to Jesus's disciples, they are for us as well. In the second chapter of Acts, we'll see the Spirit fall upon the new church—and we are now representatives of that same church, blessedly infilled by the Spirit of God.

Lord, thank you for sending your Spirit. I know I need help in discerning truth from error. I certainly need an advocate when things go awry in my life. I need guidance and daily encouragement. Thank you that I can easily find that in your Spirit within. Amen.

GOD GOES FISHING

○ **Morning:** John 19–21
○ **Noon:** Luke 1–5
○ **Night:** Psalms 110–112

There's a beautiful bookending to a story told in three Gospels. In Matthew 4:18–20 we saw an encounter between Jesus and Simon (Peter) and Simon's brother Andrew. Jesus walks along the shoreline of the Sea of Galilee while the two are fishing. He calls over to them and asks them to follow him, and if they will, he will show them "how to fish for people!" (v. 19). They left everything and followed Jesus.

In another instance in Luke 5:4–11, Jesus tells the beleaguered fishermen, who have been up all night and caught nothing, to let down their nets for a catch. They obey Jesus, then catch so many fish that their nets threaten to break. In this story, the calling to fish for people comes at the very end.

After Jesus's death and resurrection, there's a reunion of sorts with the same beginning-of-ministry setting in John 21. We see Jesus on Galilee's beach and the fishermen doing what they did prior to meeting Jesus. Again, they had caught nothing, though they fished all night. Jesus says almost the same words he did in the beginning. "Throw out your net on the right-hand side of the boat, and you'll get some," he says (John 21:6). Of course, they experienced the same abundance of fish—overwhelmingly so.

John, known as "the disciple Jesus loved (see John 13:23 and 21:20), exclaims that it was the Lord who gave the fishing advice. Peter swims and then runs toward the Lord on the shore, where a meal of fish and bread awaited. Imagine that—the bread of life offering bread, the one who proclaimed his disciples would be fishers of men now providing fish as sustenance!

After this, there's an important scene between Jesus and Peter, who denied him thrice. Jesus restored Peter by asking him three times, "Do you love me?" Peter, distressed the third time, exclaims, "Lord, you know everything. You know that I love you" (John 21:17). Three times Jesus instructed Peter to take care of lambs and sheep—to feed, take care of, and tend to the sheep in his care.

To be a fisher of people is to love them, shepherd them, and feed them. We begin the story of the disciples with food (fish!), and we end it the same way. It is our job as disciples to fish for others (to pursue!) and to tend to them once they've met Jesus (to shepherd!).

Lord, thank you for how beautifully these stories interweave with one another. Help me to no longer be afraid to tell others about you. And, like Peter, I want to be someone who tends to the needs of others and shepherds them well. Help me to do that in my life today. Amen.

GOD TELLS PARABLES

○ **Morning:** Luke 6–9
○ **Noon:** Luke 10–13
○ **Night:** Psalms 113–115

Luke, this book's author, also wrote the book of Acts. Throughout both books, you see a lot of storytelling. The most parables (stories) you'll see in any of the Gospels are found in the book of Luke. Jesus gives us a glimpse of why he taught this way in Matthew 13:35, when he directly quotes Psalm 78:2, "For I will speak to you in a parable. I will teach you hidden lessons from our past."

A parable is a story with layered meanings. It typically came from an everyday occurrence or item—a coin, a widow, workers in the field, the building of barns, sheep, children going astray, crops, or pearls. Parables, because of this, were inherently relatable, but were not always discernable on the surface. Jesus said to his disciples, "You are permitted to understand the secrets of the Kingdom of God. But I use parables to teach the others so that the Scriptures might be fulfilled" (Luke 8:10), followed by a quote from Isaiah 6:9 about looking yet not seeing, hearing but not understanding.

Right after that, Jesus pulls back the curtain of a famous parable's meaning. Let's dig into the parable of the soils.

By now you've read a large portion of the Bible, and you're making strong connections between the Old and New Testaments. You know that God's heart has always been to bring all people to himself. Therefore, reading this parable may take on new meaning.

The farmer, Jesus tells us, scatters the Word of God as seed—and that seed has four possible outcomes. The field is the world, and it hosts different soils—an exposed footpath, rocky soil, some thorny dirt, and soil with good tilth. The first three seeds don't grow to maturity. They're either snatched up, shallow-rooted and wilted, or choked of life. Only the good soil produces an amazing crop.

So it is with our world today. While we cannot control the soil of others' lives, we can follow the example of the farmer and cast our seeds, hoping and praying that those seeds will take root and grow. The outcome is up to the Lord. All we can do is obey the Father's heart to share his great news with others. This is our kingdom work. What a privilege to be a part of God's great redemption of humankind!

> Lord, help me to scatter seeds, trusting in you to help those seeds find the right soil. I pray for those who have been snatched away by the devil. Please rescue! And for those with no root, I pray you'd lengthen their roots. For those choked by this world, release its grip. Amen.

✓ Day 69

GOD SUFFERS

○ **Morning:** Luke 14–18
○ **Noon:** Luke 19–22
○ **Night:** Psalms 116–117

It's hard to imagine the supreme suffering Jesus endured for our sake. Imagine pouring into another human being (Judas Iscariot) when you know he will betray you. Imagine what it must've felt like to watch Judas walk away, intent on that betrayal.

Think about Jesus having a final meal with his friends, realizing that they'd all scatter and that one of his closest would deny him three times. What would it have been like to be so lonely as Jesus prayed that the cup of God's suffering would pass from him, only to find his companions asleep?

To be kissed during betrayal, to see the angry mob with clubs and swords coming near you, to be falsely accused. To have every ill motive (all untrue) assigned to you by the very people who were supposed to "get" you—imagine how devastating that would be.

Although Jesus was the King of kings and Lord of lords, his people mocked him, tortured him, and beat him bloody. They blasphemed him. How perplexing that even the Roman authorities found no fault in him, yet his people assigned all fault to him.

Instead of a crown befitting a king, Jesus wore a circle of thorns, piercing his head while blood ran to the earth. Roman soldiers flogged him, ripping flesh with each blow. Not only that, but the people who experienced Jesus's healings, miracles, and resurrections, who shouted *hosanna*, now screamed *crucify*. In his stead, the murderer Barabbas was set free.

At the place of the skull, Jesus endured his torturous death among criminals. His wrists and ankles nailed to a cross beam, he had to pull himself up on those spikes to grab a quick breath. Jesus suffocated. He bled. His heart melted within him.

When he breathed his last, of course darkness covered the earth. The author of life was dead, and the sky responded by mourning in shrouded darkness.

This is the sacrifice our Lord made for us, bearing the weight of humanity's sin upon that horrible instrument of torture. If you ever doubt God's love for you, read afresh these difficult accounts. This is what love looks like. This crucifixion and subsequent resurrection are the climax of the story of the Bible, where God did what humanity could not—rescue, atone, redeem.

Lord, "thank you" seems so small. You endured ridicule, mockery, and pain for me, for us, for this world you love. Thank you for the cross. Thank you for your willingness to endure it. Thank you for your fidelity to the plan of God. I'm forever grateful. Amen.

✓ Day 70

GOD CREATES THE CHURCH

○ **Morning:** Luke 23–24
○ **Noon:** Acts 1–6
○ **Night:** Psalm 118

Many scholars call the books of Luke and Acts *Luke-Acts* since they were penned by the same author, the physician Luke. Acts, then, is the continuation of the story of Jesus. In fact, we see an encounter with Jesus in the first chapter of Acts prior to the ascension. Here Jesus tells the disciples to stay in Jerusalem, then utters these beautifully prophetic words, "But you will receive power when the Holy Spirit comes upon you. And you will be my witnesses, telling people about me everywhere—in Jerusalem, throughout Judea, in Samaria, and to the ends of the earth" (Acts 1:8). Can you see the heart of God in these verses? His longing has always been to bring the whole world to himself.

Even more interesting is the scene in chapter 2 when the Holy Spirit falls upon the believers who are gathered. Around Jerusalem were people who represented all the languages Jesus just talked about—Jews, Samaritans, Gentiles. When the disciples began speaking in other foreign tongues, the people surrounding them were amazed. "These people are all from Galilee, and yet we hear them speaking in our own native languages!" (Acts 2:7–8).

You may remember way back in Genesis 11 a different kind of language phenomenon. The world at that time spoke the same language. The people gathered and tried to build a tower to God in their own strength. God then confused the languages of the people and scattered them throughout the earth. We see a sinful people disbursed.

But in today's story of the birth of the church, we see the opposite. We see God coming down to earth, giving people languages of the world, gathering people from every tribe, tongue, and nation into a unified body.

During the tower of Babel, we see unified sinfulness. During the Holy Spirit's falling, we see unified diversity and holiness.

Peter, after this powerful demonstration of the Spirit's language in tongues of fire, quotes Joel 2:28–32 about God's Spirit pouring radically on all people. Young and old will experience miracles. Men and women will be welcomed to the table of the righteous. The passage ends with, "But everyone who calls on the name of the LORD will be saved" (Acts 2:21).

Jesus's life, death, and resurrection represent a turning point in history on which everything pivots. His is the great reversal—what is lost is found, what is scattered is gathered, what is not understood is discerned. Because of this, we all have a fixed hope that cannot be moved. If Jesus can reverse the curse of Babel and the penalty of sin and death, then surely he can rescue us—as long as we call upon the name of the Lord.

Lord, I call on you right now. I am humbled and grateful that you reversed Babel and brought language to the disciples from all over the world, revealing your heart for everyone, including me. What a powerful connection! I love you, and I worship you. Amen.

GOD SAVES A SINNER

○ **Morning:** Acts 7–10
○ **Noon:** Acts 11–14
○ **Night:** Psalm 119:1–80

What a beautiful believer Stephen was. As he breathed his last as people stoned him, he made a startling exclamation—that he saw the Son of Man (Jesus) *standing* at the right hand of the Father. Normally a sovereign would sit at the right hand, but Jesus *stood* to welcome Stephen the martyr into glory.

The next verse we read is Acts 8:1. "Saul was one of the witnesses, and he agreed completely with the killing of Stephen."

Have you ever despaired of someone you love ever finding Jesus? Saul was someone who appeared to be beyond the reach of God— murdering Jesus's followers seems to deem him irredeemable. At the hands of Saul, persecution flourished. In some ways, this was horrible (of course), but God used that persecution to do precisely what he had in mind all along—to bring the nations to himself. This diaspora caused people to leave the comfort of Jerusalem and take their newfound faith all around the Roman Empire and beyond.

Amid this persecution, we find Acts chapter 9, where the miraculous happens. This should encourage us that God will do anything to bring even the greatest enemy of the gospel to himself. Saul-then-Paul's conversion involves the miraculous. He who thought he saw the truth so clearly is blinded by the One who is truth personified. Jesus asks him a powerful question, "Why are you persecuting me?" (Acts 9:4).

Saul, who thought he was loving God, must come to the realization that, no, he was actually persecuting God.

And as we look at Paul's life, we see he will follow in the same footsteps of the One who blinded him. He, too, will be persecuted frequently. He will suffer for the sake of the kingdom of God.

In addition, Paul will count everything prestigious he enjoyed as a religious elite as sheer garbage for the sake of knowing Jesus Christ and him crucified. He will eat his words, apologize for his pre-conversion life, and spend his last years on earth starting churches, facing dangers, and writing a significant portion of the New Testament.

This is the power of the gospel in action—taking a hater of the church and transforming him into a builder of the body of Christ. If Saul can find Jesus, there is always hope for those in your life who are far from him. Don't give up. Keep praying. Continue to trust that God is able to rescue even the person who seems farthest away.

Lord, wow. You saved a notorious sinner, a persecutor of the church. Nothing is impossible for you. So, would you please draw those who are far from you to yourself? Would you rescue those I love? Thank you in advance for what you do. Amen.

Day 72

GOD SENDS MISSIONARIES

○ **Morning:** Acts 15–18
○ **Noon:** Acts 19–22
○ **Night:** Psalm 119:81–144

Throughout the book of Acts, you'll encounter several missionary journeys of Paul, but you'll also see people everywhere sharing the message of the Good News. What a powerful expansion of the kingdom, often through supernatural means. In chapter 16, we see a unique alliance forming between Paul and Timothy. Together, they traveled throughout the empire in a father-son bond, with Paul discipling the young Timothy, training him to plant and establish churches.

If you look closely, you'll see a pronoun shift in the narrative. Luke had used *they* and *them* to describe a journey, but in Acts 16:10, he switches to *we* and *us*. "So *we* decided to leave for Macedonia at once, having concluded that God was calling *us* to preach the Good News there" (emphases mine). This is because Luke the physician joined Paul and Silas on their missionary journey.

In a style like Jesus's, the apostles first entered a city and went into the synagogues to teach and persuade people to meet Jesus. In some cities, there were no synagogues, so groups of people would meet for prayer.

This is how the church in Philippi started—on a riverbank with a group of women praying. Lydia was one of those women. She listened to the apostle's message, believed, then was baptized in the same river. Her conversion reminds us that the kingdom of God is not merely for Jewish men, but for women too.

The book of Acts is a roadmap for all the epistles later. A fascinating practice when you're not rapid-reading the Bible is to locate the place in Acts where each church began and read that prior to picking up the epistle of the same locale. Throughout Acts, we see churches planted in Corinth, Philippi (as in the case of Lydia), Thessalonica, Ephesus, Galatia, and Colossae, among other places.

There's a bookending that happens when Paul travels away from his church-planting efforts to return to Jerusalem. There he addresses many Jewish people, testifying to Jesus's rescue of him. In the place he used to kill Christians he is now bringing the message of life. Where Stephen "gazed steadily" (see Acts 7:55) toward the sky before his martyrdom, Paul now is "gazing intently at the high council" (Acts 23:1). Both men have been utterly transformed by Jesus Christ, and both are unafraid to testify about him.

Lord, thank you for your kindness toward me. Thank you for sending people my way when I needed to know about you. I want to be available to share you boldly wherever you send me. I realize I'm a missionary right where I am. Empower me. Amen.

Day 73

GOD REVEALS OUR HEARTS

○ **Morning:** Acts 23–28
○ **Noon:** Romans 1–2
○ **Night:** Psalm 119:145–176

If you want to have a significant experience of the book of Romans, read Exodus just prior. Of course, that's not easy to do when you're rapid-reading the Bible, but the next time through, consider doing this. Why? Because you cannot understand the message of Romans fully without first understanding the exodus and God's great deliverance of the nation of Israel.

You will see so much emancipation language in Romans, about people enslaved being set free from the shackles of oppression. Just as God delivered the Israelites from Egypt, through Jesus he delivered us from the domain and power of sin (which is its own slavery) into the kingdom of his marvelous light. Darkness to light. Slavery to freedom. Fear to confidence. Confusion to clarity.

But before we can shout amen to the beauty of the gospel, the apostle Paul must first take us on a trip through history, revealing humanity's propensity for sin. If we don't know we have a fatal sin problem, we won't see our need for a savior.

Paul paints a bleak picture of a godless people who, although they saw the handiwork of God in creation, chose instead to worship things on earth. Because of this, they have no excuse because God has revealed himself to everyone. Paul writes, "Yes, they knew God, but they wouldn't worship him as God or even give him thanks. And they began to think up foolish ideas of what God was like. As a result, their minds became dark and confused. Claiming to be wise, they instead became utter fools. And instead of worshiping the glorious, ever-living God, they worshiped idols made to look like mere people and birds and animals and reptiles" (Romans 1:21–23).

Perhaps the scariest phrase in the New Testament comes in the following verse. "So God abandoned them to do whatever shameful things their hearts desired" (Romans 1:24). The God who loved humankind chose to abandon people to their own vices. Why? Because God is not an autocrat out to control people for his own pleasure. In his love, he grants us freedom to choose. And sometimes that means humanity chooses sin.

Paul continues his foray into sin and oppression by moving from the whole world to the nation of Israel. They are not immune from depravity. In chapter 2, he exposes the hypocrisy of the Jewish people, who consider themselves "a guide for the blind" (see Romans 2:19). They do the very things they tell others not to do. He concludes by saying it's not the façade of Judaism or even their heritage that makes one a true Jew, but it's their heart. "No, a true Jew is one whose heart is right with God" (Romans 2:29).

Therefore, we are all painted by sin's brushstroke. We, Jew and Gentile alike, need rescue from our slavery to sin.

Lord, I recognize my propensity for sin. I see how many times I've run to created things instead of to you, the Creator. Please forgive me. I want to have a heart that beats for you. I want to chase after your ways. I need you, Lord. Amen.

GOD REQUIRES BELIEF

○ **Morning:** Romans 3–7
○ **Noon:** Romans 8–10
○ **Night:** Psalms 120–121

Romans is a meaty book full of profound truths about the Good News and our daily lives as followers of Jesus. The apostle Paul lays out the need for Jesus (all have sinned), the means to deal with sin (a sinless Jesus takes the place of sinful humanity as a sacrifice), and the hope we have as followers of Jesus (the resurrection gives us a living, vital hope both in this life and the next). And peppered throughout the narrative is this idea of belief, or faith.

God requires our faith. We must trust that he did what he said he did. We must believe in the saving power of the cross and the power of the resurrection. Without belief, we tend to look to laws to follow by rote, which then leaves us despondent (we can't do it all!) or proud (we are awesome!).

Paul lays out very plainly how we who are sinners can be reconciled to a holy God. "For God presented Jesus as the sacrifice for sin. People are made right with God when they believe that Jesus sacrificed his life, shedding his blood. This sacrifice shows that God was being fair when he held back and did not punish those who sinned in times past" (Romans 3:25). We are made right as we believe. He continues, "Can we boast, then, that we have done anything to be accepted by God? No, because our acquittal is not based on obeying the law. It is based on faith" (Romans 3:27).

Abraham demonstrated this belief in eons past when he truly believed the covenant of God to make him into a great nation. There's a beautiful verse tucked into Romans 4 that reveals the why of faith. "Clearly, God's promise to give the whole earth to

Abraham and his descendants was based not on his obedience to God's law, but on a right relationship with God that comes by faith" (Romans 4:13). The truth: Having belief springs from a robust relationship.

Think about it this way. Let's say there is a person you have never met who approaches you and asks you to travel with them across the country. It would be unwise to do so because you truly do not know that person. They could be nefarious or have ill intentions. To have faith in that stranger would be foolhardy.

But if it's your best friend who wants to road-trip with you, you are apt to say yes (if you have the time and means). Why? Because you know that person intimately. You can easily put trust in them because of your shared relationship.

Trust is based on relationship. If you struggle to trust God, it simply means you have more to know about him because to know him is to believe his good intentions toward us.

> *Lord, I love how uncomplicated the gospel is. I simply believe that you are good because I've experienced you as good. I choose to trust you because you are trustworthy. I choose to believe you because you have never let me down. Thank you for the gospel. Amen.*

GOD GIVES GUIDANCE

○ **Morning:** Romans 11–16
○ **Noon:** 1 Corinthians 1–2
○ **Night:** Psalms 122–123

If you ask Christ-followers, many cite Romans 12 as their favorite chapter in the Bible. Why is that? It's practical, and it offers clear guidance on how we should live as followers of Christ.

In fact, every time you run across guidance like this in the New Testament (the Sermon on the Mount, for instance), it's an interesting practice to view those guidelines through the framework of the Ten Commandments. There we learn how to treat God and love each other. Romans 12 is no different.

Paul reminds his brothers and sisters in the beginning of the chapter how we are to relate to our God. We are to remember the sacrificial system of the Old Testament and offer our lives and bodies to him as our spiritual act of service. In other words, God gets all of us. A sacrifice is consumed wholly—there are no parts left.

Next Paul shares about the importance of our thought lives. How we think is how we end up living, so he encourages believers to pay more attention to God and his ways than the world and its siren calls.

Just as the Ten Commandments switch from our relationship to God toward our relationship to others, Paul shifts his focus after verse 3. In order to have thriving relationships on this earth, we must be humble. We should exercise any gift God has given us with the higher ethic of serving each other, being grateful for the diversity of gifts God gives his people.

He commands us to really love each other, not merely give lip service. He tips us toward generosity, to work hard so we can meet the needs of others. He reminds us to keep on praying, even when we don't see answers. When others harm us, God calls us to bless them instead. Perhaps the most profound relational advice comes in Romans 12:15, "Be happy with those who are happy, and weep with those who weep." To truly rejoice in someone's victory is a hallmark of good friendship. To be able to cry alongside a grieving friend is to enter their grief—it's what Jesus would do.

Paul ends this powerful chapter by talking about vengeance—that it is always God's to dole out, not our prerogative. We must trust that God can right every wrong. To not retaliate (when we truly feel like doing so) is to trust God's perfect justice and timing. The end of the chapter sums up what creates relational harmony: "Don't let evil conquer you, but conquer evil by doing good" (Romans 12:21).

Lord, thank you for the profound harmony of Scripture, for how this chapter mirrors the Ten Commandments to love you and love others. I give you those difficult parts of my story where I'm hurting from the acts of others. Help me entrust those feelings and people fully to you. Amen.

GOD EMPOWERS RELATIONSHIPS

○ **Morning:** 1 Corinthians 3–5
○ **Noon:** 1 Corinthians 6–10
○ **Night:** Psalms 124–125

When we read the epistles (which simply means letters), we must remember that these books are not simply theological treatises written for all time (though they are that as well). These are letters written to specific communities of people with problems aplenty. These letters are a glimpse into the embryonic church living amidst a pagan culture. In that sense, these become universal letters to help us, since all human beings are messy and make messes of things.

This was true in the Corinthian church, which was mired in sexual sin that had not been addressed, believers taking each other to court, confusion about what to do about sacrificial meat, and the problem of disunity. Paul had firm words for the believers there, always underlining the importance of living in relationship.

Paul has the right to speak plainly because his relationship with the Corinthian church is one of father to children. He writes, "For even if you had ten thousand others to teach you about Christ, you have only one spiritual father. For I became your father in Christ Jesus when I preached the Good News to you" (1 Corinthians 4:15). So, as a loving father, he confronts a disordered relationship in which a man is having sex with his stepmother. He urges them to do the right thing by confronting this man and taking this sin seriously. In 2 Corinthians, you'll see the result of Paul's advice (and it turns out for the better).

He cautions against lawsuits among fellow believers, then urges his listeners to flee from sexual sin. He reminds the Corinthians that they are parts of Jesus Christ: "Should a man take his body, which is part of Christ, and join it to a prostitute? Never!" (1 Corinthians 6:15). And then he speaks of marriage, of its sober vow, and how singleness is a beautiful means of serving God.

He finishes speaking about relationships by reminding the Corinthian church to give up their rights for each other. This is not something Paul simply preaches but does not practice. "Even though I am a free man with no master, I have become a slave to all people to bring many to Christ" (1 Corinthians 9:19). His heartbeat was to lay down his life and rights so that many would come to know Jesus as Lord and Savior.

This evangelistic desire undergirds all of Paul's letters. He longs to see the completion of what God promised to Abraham millennia ago—that the whole world would know the one true God and worship him with joyful abandon. Though he longed for the Corinthian believers to have right relationships with each other, he longed even more that all people would be in a right relationship with their Creator.

Lord, wow. Thank you for caring about my relationships. Help me remember that I am not my own; I've been bought with a price, so I want to glorify you in my closest, most fundamental relationships. But even more, I want to revere you as my king. Amen.

GOD GRANTS GIFTS

○ **Morning:** 1 Corinthians 11–16
○ **Noon:** 2 Corinthians 1–2
○ **Night:** Psalms 126–127

To bless the body of Christ, God gave each person gifts to use—not for their own glory, but for the building up of the church. How amazing that God would entrust ministry to us, his people. He didn't have to do that. But he knew that building the kingdom was a joyful endeavor, so he empowered us to work with him as we love others.

In chapter 12 of 1 Corinthians, we see these gifts delineated. There are several different parts of Scripture that talk about spiritual gifts, including Romans 12 (that we read just two days ago), Ephesians 4, and 1 Peter 4. The purpose of these gifts is to help build up the church, so they are outwardly focused, for the sake of everyone.

Paul wants to reiterate that there is one Holy Spirit who gives these gifts graciously, and just because they're different doesn't mean the Spirit is many parts. He is one; his gifts are varied. Similarly, the church of Jesus Christ should be one in unity, but our roles are varied. This is a good thing because the Spirit knows best what each local church needs, and he arranges us as he sees fit. Here Paul uses the metaphor of a body to describe a church. "But our bodies have many parts, and God has put each part just where he wants it" (1 Corinthians 12:18).

Did you know that God promises each of us a gift? "A spiritual gift is given to each of us so we can help each other" (1 Corinthians 12:7). He gives believers wisdom, knowledge, faith, healings, miracles, prophesies, discernment, unknown tongues, and the interpretation of those tongues. He gives people the ability to helm the church as apostles, prophets, teachers, helpers, and leaders. Together, in this beautiful, varied body of Christ, we serve each other and help each other grow to maturity.

Gifts are graces God grants us. They are not to be hoarded or leveraged for our own personal gain. They are meant to empower us to serve, to take the last seat, to wash the feet of those who are broken.

Tucked away in 1 Corinthians 12 is an admonition to remember those who seem less worthy of gifts, or those whose gifts seem small. "So God has put the body together such that extra honor and care are given to those parts that have less dignity. This makes for harmony among the members, so that all the members care for each other" (1 Corinthians 12:24–25). If we have outward gifts that everyone can see, it just means that we use them to serve those who are unseen. This Scripture reminds us to dignify those who don't have a voice or a place at the table. At the foot of the cross, we are all level. Under the holy gaze of God, we are all paupers. No one is greater than the other.

> *Lord, thank you for putting the body together in such a way that makes for kindness and service to reign. Help me employ the gifts you've given me to serve those who are unnoticed. Thank you for not having favorites, and for your design where everyone plays an important role. Amen.*

GOD MAKES US NEW

○ **Morning:** 2 Corinthians 3–6
○ **Noon:** 2 Corinthians 7–10
○ **Night:** Psalms 128–129

To be reconciled is to have our broken relationships restored. When Jesus, sinless, went to the cross on our behalf, he made friends of enemies. Those who were sinners (all of us), alienated from a holy God, could now approach the throne of grace with confidence. Our familial relationship with God the Father is now restored because of Christ's sacrifice, and that relationship can now commence and flourish.

All that we once were is in the past. All our propensity toward sin has been dealt a deathly blow through Christ's death on a tree. Our old way of doing life has also been crucified along with Christ. Becoming a Christ-follower means leaving the old behind and embracing the amazing life Jesus has secured for us.

There is a profound shift when a person moves from unbelief to belief. Paul summarizes it this way: "Since we believe that Christ died for all, we also believe that we have all died to our old life. He died for everyone so that those who receive his new life will no longer live for themselves. Instead, they will live for Christ, who died and was raised for them" (2 Corinthians 5:14–15). The gospel is neatly delineated in those verses. We had an old life of sin that we lived in self-absorption. Jesus died and resurrected so that we could shift from living solely for ourselves and our pleasure toward wholly living for Jesus Christ.

Following that statement is one of the most memorized verses in the Bible, for good reason because it involves a powerful promise. "This means that anyone who belongs to Christ has become a new person. The old life is gone; a new life has begun!" (2 Corinthians 5:17). What a joy! What we were is no longer who we are today. From dead to alive, broken to healed, enslaved to free!

But this new life has a task attached to it. To be new is to become a part of God's reconciliation plan for humankind. What a privilege! Paul calls us ambassadors in this sense. "So we are Christ's ambassadors; God is making his appeal through us. We speak for Christ when we plead, 'Come back to God!'" (2 Corinthians 5:20). An ambassador is someone who lives in another country but represents the country she came from. Similarly, we who are made new represent our ultimate home, heaven, while we are exiled on this earth. Because we are made incredibly new by the life, death, and resurrection of Jesus Christ, we have a holy obligation to tell others of the gift God gives us.

Who, in your life, needs that kind of reconciliation? Who needs to be made new?

Lord, I pray for the people in my life who are not yet reconciled to you. They don't realize their need for a relationship with you. They're lost and broken. Would you empower me to be a good ambassador of your kingdom? Show me how to love them well today. Amen.

GOD GIVES STRENGTH

○ **Morning:** 2 Corinthians 11–13
○ **Noon:** Galatians 1–6
○ **Night:** Psalms 130–131

In 2 Corinthians 12, we learn of something painful Paul has had to endure. He calls it a thorn in his flesh—"a messenger from Satan to torment me and keep me from becoming proud" (v. 7). Some have speculated this was a person. Others have pointed to a possible eye condition that was unrelenting. That the thorn is not named makes it universally relatable to us all. At any point in time, we can experience something that pokes at us, tormenting us without reason.

Thankfully, we see Paul's humanity in this passage. He does ask God to take it away—three times. The word used in the NLT in verse 8 is *begged*. Paul truly was pierced by this thorn. Have you been in that place of desperation with a person or a situation in your life? For whatever reason, God does not take away the pain, but allows it to stay.

What Paul does next is constructive. He listens to the voice of God, who utters a powerful truth: "My grace is all you need. My power works best in weakness" (v. 9). After this, Paul makes a mental U-turn. He shifts from begging to boasting. Now he sees the thorn as a means to understand this paradoxical equation: His weakness = God's strength.

His reversal is extreme, actually. "That's why I take pleasure in my weaknesses, and in the insults, hardships, persecutions, and troubles that I suffer for Christ. For when I am weak, then I am strong" (v. 10). To take pleasure in all those trials meant that something supernatural had taken place. God gave Paul the ability to smile when difficulties came—not because he was masochistic, but because he understood that when life pressed in on him, it would require him to rely more heavily on the strength God supplied.

When we live life in our own strength and things are going well, we feel we have no need of the Lord. Trials and difficulties are gifts in disguise because they help us realize our weakness and our constant need for Jesus. When we think of pride, we picture someone with their nose in the air, looking down on others. But the root of pride is self-sufficiency. It's saying, "I can do this all on my own, thank you very much."

I often think of the J.B. Phillips translation of James 1:2 where he equates trials with friends, "When all kinds of trials and temptations crowd into your lives my brothers, don't resent them as intruders, but welcome them as friends!" These trials are tutors toward the strength that God graciously supplies. Without them, we may not reach for the One who is strong.

Lord, when I think of the apostle Paul, I think of strength. But thank you for reminding me that he was a human being like me, bothered by trials, and in need of you. I choose to recognize my weakness. Please provide the strength I need today. Amen.

✓ Day 80

GOD OFFERS GRACE

- ○ **Morning:** Ephesians 1–6
- ○ **Noon:** Philippians 1–2
- ○ **Night:** Psalms 132–133

Can you believe that after today's reading, you are ten days away from finishing this Bible-in-ninety-days challenge? I'm so proud of your tenacity and endurance! What a feat! I pray you have a confident grasp of the narrative of Scripture because of this challenge.

Both letters you are reading today, like many of Paul's, are written from prison, which gives each one a certain gravitas. These are the words of a church planter and missionary whose heart bleeds for the churches left behind. You can hear the shepherd heart as you read Paul's words—he has a strong desire to see each church grow up, be discipled, and make an impact for the kingdom.

In Ephesians, he lays out the gospel in simple yet profound terms, reiterating that this gift is not merely for the Jew, but for the Gentile as well—Good News for all. And undergirding this good news is the concept of grace.

The Greek word Paul uses for grace is a common one, *chariti*. This looks an awful lot like our word *charity*, which means giving something necessary to someone in need. That captures a lot of the nuance of God's grace to us. It is unmerited, meaning we don't deserve such kindness. The charitable act of God is nondependent on our goodness, but it's steeped in his benevolence. Just as there's a power dynamic in charitable work (an institution or individual helps someone who cannot help themselves), our all-powerful God graces us who have no power to conquer our sin.

Another one of those famous, memorized verses highlights this grace. "God saved you by his grace when you believed. And you can't take credit for this; it is a gift from God. Salvation is not a reward for the good things we have done, so none of us can boast about it" (Ephesians 2:8–9). God is the giver of this indescribable, undeserved gift.

What should our response be to this profound kindness?

Gratitude. Did you know that *thanksgiving*, *grace*, and *joy* are in the same family of words? Our response to being graced by God is to be gracious receivers, utterly thankful and full of praise. We did not deserve such a reversal. Yet God, in his forethought, chose us before the world's foundation to be accepted and invited into his family. We once were far away, but now we are near. We once were alienated, but now we are family. All because of grace.

This grace enables us to be gracious and charitable toward others. If we've been so graced, surely we can be transformed by it in the way we treat others. To be graced is to become a grace giver.

Lord, how can I ever thank you for gracing me with this life? Thank you for bringing me into your family as your child. Thank you for doing what I could not. Thank you for your kindness toward me, a person once enslaved by sin. I'm so grateful. Amen.

Day 81

GOD HOLDS ALL THINGS TOGETHER

○ **Morning:** Philippians 3–4
○ **Noon:** Colossians 1–4 and 1 Thessalonians 1–2
○ **Night:** Psalms 134–135

Most of the New Testament is written in prose. It has poetic passages, but they are mainly quotations from the Old Testament, and you find poetic structure in the prophetic book of Revelation. Occasionally you'll see poetry in the rest of the New Testament that stands on its own. Colossians 1:15–20 is one of these passages.

Here Paul is believed to be quoting a hymn sung by the early church, which is why it is written in stanza format. He is applying the words to the church in Colossae's situation—it would be like using the words of a modern worship song to bring gentle correction to a particular church that failed to live up to its lyrics.

This song is powerful, rich in theology.

Here we learn that Jesus is God in the flesh, that he created everything we see and everything we can't see. The unseen world of power (thrones, kingdoms) is his as well. Jesus has always existed, and he now is the head of the church (you and me!). He is the beginning of all things, greater than all because of his resurrection. He is the reconciler of humankind to God the Father. He is the ultimate peacemaker between heaven and earth. All this happened because of his death on the cross, where he shed his blood for us all.

But there's a little phraseology tucked into this song that may bring you comfort today. It's this: "He holds all creation together" (Colossians 1:17). Do you ever feel like life is chaotic and cruel? Have you had it with all the pain you've experienced of late? Do events seem arbitrary? Have you suffered in your mental health, or has someone you loved battled depression or suicidal thoughts? Has a health scare immobilized you?

There is hope.

Even when the world shifts on its axis and our circumstances tend toward dire, our God is on the throne, holding all creation together. That creation is not merely mountains or weather or the heavens above. That creation includes you. He holds *you* together.

If you're struggling today, the God who holds you has prompted Paul to pray for you. Let these words wash over you: "We ask God to give you complete knowledge of his will and to give you spiritual wisdom and understanding. Then the way you live will always honor and please the Lord, and your lives will produce every kind of good fruit. All the while, you will grow as you learn to know God better and better. We also pray that you will be strengthened with all his glorious power so you will have all the endurance and patience you need. May you be filled with joy, always thanking the Father" (Colossians 1:9–12).

> Lord, I need you to hold me together. Thank you for poetically reminding me that you are everything, and you are worthy of my allegiance. I give you all the things on my mind today, including broken dreams and relationships. Hold me together, I pray. Amen.

Day 82

GOD PREPARES US FOR THE END

- ○ **Morning:** 1 Thessalonians 3–5
- ○ **Noon:** 2 Thessalonians 1–3 and 1 Timothy 1–2
- ○ **Night:** Psalms 136–137

We all die. While that's not fun to think about, it is a universal truth—something even Jesus did. But what happens after death? And how does God prepare us for our home beyond the grave? In today's reading, you read about the Day of the Lord. This is not merely a New Testament phenomenon, but it was addressed and predicted throughout the Old Testament. It's also called the Day of Yahweh.

Zephaniah predicted doom when he described this day. "It will be a day when the LORD's anger is poured out—a day of terrible distress and anguish, a day of ruin and desolation, a day of darkness and gloom, a day of clouds and blackness" (Zephaniah 1:15).

But also, this: The Day of the Lord would be a day when the messiah would begin his cosmic reign. In the Old Testament, we looked forward to that moment when the messiah would be revealed. In the New Testament, we meet *the* Messiah, Jesus the Christ. The Day of the Lord for a Christ-follower is not to be feared. It simply means the moment when the kingdom of the world becomes the kingdom of Jesus.

At the end of time, Jesus will gather his people from all over the earth, including those who have died. And he will establish his kingdom. "For since we believe that Jesus died and was raised to life again, we also believe that when Jesus returns, God will bring back with him the believers who have died" (1 Thessalonians 4:14).

Paul further describes the Day of the Lord as something to be prepared for. There are many interpretations of the end times—whether there will be a rapture or not, when or whether Jesus will reign for a thousand years, who will walk through the tribulation, and when the final judgment will occur. But the thrust of Paul's message has less to do with those technicalities and more to do with our readiness.

No matter how the end of the world transpires, we are called to be prepared. "So be on your guard, not asleep like the others. Stay alert and be clearheaded" (1 Thessalonians 5:6). Whether you are confused about the timelines or worried about what will happen in the end, the good news is that Jesus died for you and has secured your place with him. Your job is simply to be obedient and watchful.

In 2 Thessalonians, Paul gives more predictors about the Day of the Lord. "For that day will not come until there is a great rebellion against God and the man of lawlessness is revealed—the one who brings destruction" (2 Thessalonians 2:3). The end will come as people on earth witness a mass apostasy. We feel inklings and pangs of that today, which means the day draws closer. There's no need to fear, thankfully, because our Messiah has conquered death, and he has already been judged for our sins. Those who are far from Christ should fear the Day of the Lord, but we have reassurance.

Lord, I don't like to think about things like this. But I trust that you have secured my place with you through your death and resurrection. Help me stay prepared, obedient, and alert today as I love the people in my life. Thank you for saving me. Amen.

GOD CALLS US TO ENDURE

○ **Morning:** 1 Timothy 3–6 and 2 Timothy 1–4
○ **Noon:** Titus 1–3
○ **Night:** Psalms 138–139

The Christian life is not easy. The moment we meet Jesus, the enemy of our souls paints a target on our hearts and lives. In fact, those who follow hard after Jesus should expect trials. Paul reminds us, "Yes, and everyone who wants to live a godly life in Christ Jesus will suffer persecution" (2 Timothy 3:12). As we see from the apostle Paul's life, as well as the other disciples' lives post-resurrection, to live for Christ is to experience trials.

How are we to endure these trials with joy?

The metaphor Paul uses here is warfare and soldiering. "Endure suffering along with me, as a good soldier of Christ Jesus" (2 Timothy 2:3). Soldiers endure hardship for the sake of the mission before them. Everything is subjugated beneath that mission. For us? Our mission is the expansion of the kingdom of God. As we participate in that, the trials we endure become secondary to the task set before us.

That isn't to say we are to be stoic, pretending these trials and pains and persecutions don't affect us. Of course, we must lament our lot, pray through our tears, and acknowledge any trauma we experience. But what keeps us steady through that grief is the knowledge that we are called to something higher, a greater calling beyond what we see and hear.

Paul reminds Timothy that there will be many barriers and obstacles in the believer's life, particularly from people who are only interested in themselves and their own selfish agendas. He gives a listing of their traits in 2 Timothy 3:2–9. They are money-centric, boastful, scoffing, disobedient, and ungrateful. They love to harm people with the way they talk. They lack self-control. They're given to cruelty, and they despise goodness. They delight in betraying those they love. They live reckless lives while they pride themselves on their behavior. They chase new teachings, have depraved minds, and what Paul calls a "counterfeit faith" (see 2 Timothy 3:8). Paul's advice? "Stay away from people like that!" (2 Timothy 3:5).

We are called to endure, not just for the sake of endurance, but to do the work of the kingdom. One of Paul's most famous verses is not merely for pastors who teach on Sunday mornings—these words are meant to be encouragement for all of us who stay away from destructive people, have a strong sense of obedience, and love the kingdom. "Preach the word of God. Be prepared, whether the time is favorable or not. Patiently correct, rebuke, and encourage your people with good teaching" (2 Timothy 4:2).

Preach the word. Endure well.

Lord, thank you for the warnings about who to hang out with. Help me sift through my relationships considering Paul's advice here. And beyond that, I pray you would help me endure the trials I'm walking through. I pray you'd help me see beyond them, so I'll keep preaching the Word. Amen.

✓ Day 84

GOD'S SON IS SUPERIOR

○ **Morning:** Philemon 1 and Hebrews 1–2
○ **Noon:** Hebrews 3–6
○ **Night:** Psalms 140–141

A great summary of the Bible comes in the first chapter of Hebrews, a book whose author is unknown. "Long ago God spoke many times and in many ways to our ancestors through the prophets. And now in these final days, he has spoken to us through his Son. God promised everything to the Son as an inheritance, and through the Son he created the universe" (Hebrews 1:1–2). You've had the privilege of reading the Bible in a truncated time period, so when you read these words, you truly understand what is going on. The Old Testament points to Jesus. The New Testament testifies to him.

The book of Hebrews is an argument for the supremacy of Jesus over any other prophet. He is greater than Adam (and is called the second Adam by Paul). He is greater than Father Abraham, though the promise to Abraham to receive the whole earth as an inheritance is fulfilled in Jesus. He is greater than the Law and Moses. In fact, Jesus is the fulfillment of the Law. The author of Hebrews writes, "But Jesus deserves far more glory than Moses, just as a person who builds a house deserves more praise than the house itself" (Hebrews 3:3).

Jesus is greater than Elijah and Elisha, than Isaiah and Jeremiah—as his ministry reflects far more power. According to the author of Hebrews, "This shows that the Son is far greater than the angels, just as the name God gave him is greater than their names" (Hebrews 1:4). Even powerful angels live in subjection to the Son of God.

Jesus is portrayed as the Creator of everything. He is God in the flesh. He sustains the universe with a word, and he is the heir of all things. He radiates glory.

It's no small thing that Jesus reigns at God's right hand. King David prophesied this when he wrote, "The LORD said to my Lord, 'Sit in the place of honor at my right hand until I humble your enemies, making them a footstool under your feet" (Psalm 110:1). This is a kingly position, and in Hebrews 2:9, we see Jesus "crowned with glory and honor."

With all that magnanimous language, let's not forget what Jesus did for us. Though he is superior, he dwelled with humankind. He empathized with us. He wore our skin, thought our thoughts, experienced our heartaches. Even though he had the rights of kingship, he shed those rights to help us. "Even though Jesus was God's Son, he learned obedience from the things he suffered" (Hebrews 5:8).

If you are suffering today, perhaps it's helpful to know the superiority of Jesus, but even more so to remember that Jesus suffered too. There's a beautiful kinship between you and him.

> *Lord, you are greater than anything I can think of. You are everything. You are powerful and beautiful. And yet you came to earth to dwell with people like me. You identified with my plight. You suffered and died so that I might live. I am utterly grateful. Amen.*

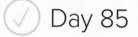

Day 85

GOD EMPOWERS PERSEVERANCE AND PATIENCE

○ **Morning:** Hebrews 7–13
○ **Noon:** James 1–3
○ **Night:** Psalms 142–143

What is faith? The Greek word used in Hebrews 11, also known as the Hall of Faith, is a common one: *pistis*. It means "conviction of the truth of anything, belief; in the NT of a conviction or belief respecting man's relationship to God and divine things . . . the conviction that God exists and is the creator and ruler of all things, the provider and bestower of eternal salvation through Christ."[1] In short, faith is believing in God's ability to run the universe without us!

Faith involves confidence in God's abilities to act, rather than placing that confidence in our own abilities. Faith also has elements of perseverance and patience in light of God's actions in the lives of his followers. That's why we see these stories in Hebrews chapter 11 of people enduring with patience the trials they walked through.

Many of the examples in this chapter did not get the answer they were looking for. They simply trusted that this life was not all there was—that one day, God would make everything right. "All these people died still believing what God had promised them. They did not receive what was promised, but they saw it all from a distance and welcomed it. They agreed that they were foreigners and nomads here on earth" (Hebrews 11:13).

The truth undergirding this kind of persevering faith is this: We were not meant for this world, and not all things will tie up perfectly in this realm. But in the other realm, where we will live forever, God will make all things right. All answered prayers will be perfectly understood. All tears will be wiped away.

In a culture that demands answers today and relief from stress in this moment, it's hard for us to be patient as we persevere. We want our answers now. But if we always received what we wanted, not only would we be spoiled believers, but we would *never* have to practice faith. Not getting everything we want is good—it helps us to have long-suffering faith, learning to believe God has good things for us as we wait.

As the author of Hebrews reminds us, "Faith shows the reality of what we hope for; it is the evidence of things we cannot see" (Hebrews 11:1). Perhaps we are weak in faith because we want our stuff now on this earth and are unwilling to persevere in patience for the intangible things God has for us in the next life.

Lord, teach me to have faith when things are not going my way. Help me to elevate my gaze from my circumstances to a future hope where everything will be made right. I want to persevere with patience because I love you and I trust you to do everything beautifully. Amen.

Day 86

GOD CAUTIONS BELIEVERS

○ **Morning:** James 4–5 and 1 Peter 1–5
○ **Noon:** 2 Peter 1–3
○ **Night:** Psalms 144–145

Apostasy and false teachers were a huge problem in the early church, and they continue to be an insidious cancer today. God cautions believers to be alert and watch out for things that do not adhere to the actual gospel.

This gospel was foreknown by God, enacted before humankind fell. Consider this powerful truth: "It was the precious blood of Christ, the sinless, spotless Lamb of God. God chose him as your ransom long before the world began, but now in these last days he has been revealed for your sake" (1 Peter 1:19–20). Before God formed the world, he had this rescue plan in mind!

That's why it's so important to protect the message of Christ. Peter, who is the author of this letter, calls Jesus the cornerstone of our faith. He breaks into song in 1 Peter 2:22–25, where he extols Jesus's sinlessness, patience, confidence, and empathy. Jesus carried our sins, heals our wounds, and shepherds our hearts.

In 2 Peter, the apostle warns us about those who would falsify the gospel. He lets the new congregation know that there will be false teachers sitting alongside them. Sadly, he predicts that many will follow these destructive teachings, and that the teachers themselves will be consumed by greed. "Many will follow their evil teaching and shameful immorality. And because of these teachers, the way of truth will be slandered. In their greed they will make up clever lies to get hold of your money. But God condemned them long ago, and their destruction will not be delayed" (2 Peter 2:2–3). We may naively think these words are for the early church, but sadly, we see these kinds of false teachers today who make money off their own followers and live lives that are unworthy to emulate. It's encouraging to know that the Lord is always cleaning house, and that these types of false teachers will be found out. Still, we are to be vigilant.

Throughout chapter 2, Peter lists qualities of false teachers who:

- Despise authority
- Are sexually promiscuous and deviant
- Are proud and arrogant
- Delight in deceiving others
- Desire sin continually
- Lure others to sin
- Are greedy
- Promise freedom, but they are slaves to sin

What a blessing that Peter gives us such a specific list!

Lord, thank you for warning me about false teachers. I know it's important not to be swayed by clever words, but to instead observe the actions of the leaders in my midst. Please give me needed discernment where I worship, I pray. Amen.

GOD IS LOVE

○ **Morning:** 1 John 1–5
○ **Noon:** 2 John and 3 John
○ **Night:** Psalm 146

John, known as the disciple Jesus loved, penned these ancient letters. Throughout each letter, the word *love* is the heartbeat of John's sentences. He paints a compelling picture of Christian community—where we live as beloved of God and that love permeates the way we treat others. Jesus made things very clear when he told us to love God first, then love others, saying those two imperatives summed up all commandments (see Matthew 22:36–40).

Love is meant to be experienced in community. We often misread much of the New Testament through individualistic lenses, including the popular 1 John 1:9 which says, "But if we confess our sins to him, he is faithful and just to forgive us our sins and to cleanse us from all wickedness." We read this that each of us individually must confess our sins, which is true. But perhaps we miss the fact that confession in these verses should be done in community—John uses the words *we* and *us* for a reason. To be a loving community does not merely mean we confess our sin quietly in our rooms, but to ask forgiveness of another, or to let your community know of your failings. That's where love can flourish, in circles of two or more.

We can live this kind of authentic love because we have experienced it first from Jesus, who died for us and invited us into his family. What a privilege it is to be known as God's very children! John writes it simply: "We know what real love is because Jesus gave up his life for us. So we also ought to give up our lives for our brothers and sisters" (1 John 3:16). In short, we experienced radical love, so we can't help but dole it out in abundant measure.

John cautions us that if we make a choice to hate someone, we are not walking in the ways of God. "If someone says, 'I love God,' but hates a fellow believer, that person is a liar; for if we don't love people we can see, how can we love God, whom we cannot see?" (1 John 4:20). Because all human beings are made in God's image (although sometimes it's hard to see), God asks us to love them. If we can't, John's argument goes, then how can we possibly love the One who created them?

To love is to fearlessly pursue another. We cannot do this of our own volition; it is something we grow into as we walk with the Lord. And in our relationship with God, we need not fear. Why? Because Jesus has already secured our place with him; we will not suffer in the judgment. "Such love has no fear, because perfect love expels all fear. If we are afraid, it is for fear of punishment, and this shows that we have not fully experienced his perfect love" (1 John 4:18). Take heart, friend. You are secure in his love for you. You have been bought, redeemed, and ushered into the family of God. So, you can love others with similar abandon.

Lord, help me to confess my sins in safe community—it's in those places I truly experience your love and forgiveness. Help me to grow in my understanding of your love for me so that it informs the way I love the people in my life, even the difficult people! Amen.

GOD SENDS WARNINGS AND ENCOURAGEMENT

○ **Morning:** Jude 1 and Revelation 1–2
○ **Noon:** Revelation 3–9
○ **Night:** Psalm 147

After reading Jude, we will conclude with the beloved disciple John's revelatory book about what to expect in the end times. This is an apocalyptic book—one that many have speculated about for millennia. Such books existed in the Old Testament as well, such as Daniel and Zechariah. The word *apocalyptic* simply means revealing or revelatory. So in this book, we see John's visions that are meant to illuminate or uncover what is to come.

Many people are afraid to read the book of Revelation, but John gives us some encouragement. "God blesses the one who reads the words of this prophecy to the church, and he blesses all who listen to its message and obey what it says, for the time is near" (Revelation 1:3). The truth? You will be blessed as you read this book. Why? Because it ends with audacious hope, a vision of our future that is wholly amazing and beautiful.

But before we get to the restoration of all things, when God comes to finally dwell with humankind forever, we must wade through warnings and cautionary tales. John begins the book with letters to seven actual churches. It's instructive to see what God warns about and what he commends or encourages.

He warns that some churches:

• Don't love as they did at first. (Ephesus)
• Tolerate bad, false teaching. (Pergamum)

- Permit a Jezebel-like prophet in their midst. (Thyatira)
- Seem alive but are actually dead. (Sardis)
- Are neither hot nor cold, but lukewarm. (Laodicea)

He commends that some churches:

- Don't tolerate evil people, and patiently suffer without quitting. (Ephesus)
- Endure suffering and poverty and opposition. (Smyrna)
- Remain loyal to God. (Pergamum)
- Have love, faith, and service. (Thyatira)
- Have not soiled their clothes. (Sardis)
- Obey God even with little strength. (Philadelphia)

We can see how important it is to be truly alive in Christ, faithfully protecting the integrity of the gospel, living rightly, weeding out heresy, and obeying God with everything inside us. Oh, that we would be found faithful as we follow Jesus!

Lord, thank you for the book of Revelation. I do pray that I will receive a blessing as I read it. Thank you for so clearly speaking to the people in those seven churches. I want to heed those cautionary tales and be a faithful, persevering follower of you! Amen.

Day 89

GOD IS WORTHY

○ **Morning:** Revelation 10–12
○ **Noon:** Revelation 13–16
○ **Night:** Psalm 148

Tucked within this apocalyptic book are hymns of praise to the greatness of God. We begin the Bible with God's magnificent power, and we end it with swirls of glory and displays of God's worthiness. He is the hero of the story of humankind, the rescuer, the One who holds the world together in his mighty grip. Because of this, he is worthy of our praise.

When the seventh trumpet sounds the third terror in chapter 11, we have an interlude of worship. In verse 15, we read that voices in heaven shouted, "The world has now become the Kingdom of our Lord and of his Christ, and he will reign forever and ever." (You may hear echoes of Handel's *Messiah* in those words!)

The world and God were united in joyful fellowship prior to the fall of humankind. God dwelt among us, and all was well. But sin caused a terrible rift between heaven and earth, God and humanity. To have all that mess finally reconciled and reunited is cause for huge celebration. Inside of us, God gives a deep longing for what should be, and we are promised that all those longings mean something and will be fulfilled when God's kingdom has fully, beautifully come to earth.

The response of the twenty-four elders in the realm of heaven is instructive for us today. First, they were sitting, but this declaration causes them to fall on their faces in worship. They say, "We give thanks to you, Lord God, the Almighty, the one who is and who always was, for now you have assumed your great power and have begun to reign" (Revelation 11:17).

We see more worship that encapsulates the Old and New Testaments wrapped up in this little verse: "And they were singing the song of Moses, the servant of God, and the song of the Lamb" (Revelation 15:3). See how the Law and the Lamb are united in one song? And that song is always praise. "Great and marvelous are your works, O Lord God, the Almighty. Just and true are your ways, O King of the nations. Who will not fear you, Lord, and glorify your name? For you alone are holy. All nations will come and worship before you, for your righteous deeds have been revealed" (Revelation 15:3–4).

God, the great Reconciler of us all, the Maker of heavens and earth, the Healer of the nations, is worthy of our worship. He has rescued us, given us a new life, adopted us as his children, and put a song of praise in our mouths. The majesty of God is on glorious display in the book of Revelation, so much so that our response should be awe and reverence.

Lord, thank you for redeeming humanity. Thank you for conquering evil. Thank you for doing such marvelous works. Thank you for being just and kind. Thank you for your unfathomable holiness, your paradoxical (but good) plan, and your heart for the world. Amen!

GOD MAKES EVERYTHING NEW

○ **Morning:** Revelation 17–20
○ **Noon:** Revelation 21–22
○ **Night:** Psalms 149–150

You have made it through the entire Bible in ninety days. What a feat! Take a moment to rejoice.

Even so, are you weary? Heavyhearted? Broken by the world? That's normal. This world is not where we are meant to dwell for eternity. God created us for himself and for another world. When we find our identity in him, we begin to find our eternal home. And in that home, all pain will be abolished.

All will be well, even if all is not well for you today. God will make everything new. A new heavens. A new earth. A new you. A new ethic of love. No more death. No more weeping. No more angst. "I heard a loud shout from the throne, saying, 'Look, God's home is now among his people! He will live with them, and they will be his people. God himself will be with them. He will wipe every tear from their eyes, and there will be no more death or sorrow or crying or pain. All these things are gone forever'" (Revelation 21:3–4). God will be with us. We will be finally free.

Coursing through the New Jerusalem will be a river of life with trees flanking it. Do you catch the imagery here? Humanity fell by grasping the fruit of a tree, and now there is a "tree of life, bearing twelve crops of fruit, with a fresh crop each month. The leaves were used for medicine to heal the nations" (Revelation 22:2).

Darkness will be abolished because Jesus will illuminate everything. He is "the bright morning star" (Revelation 22:16). Not only that, but we will see his face for eternity—the one we have loved from afar will be near us. All sin will be abolished. All grace will abound. All those who have died in Christ will reunite with one another. There will be a marriage supper, a celebration, and we will live finally healed and set free. I can imagine dancing!

We see the words of Jesus in the last chapter of Revelation. Jesus continues to warn the church that he is coming soon—he says it three times. With that imminent return, how are we to live? We must be ready, open, and on alert.

Jesus also says this: "I am the Alpha and the Omega, the First and the Last, the Beginning and the End" (Revelation 22:13). If you want to understand the story of Scripture, Jesus is the answer. He started everything, and he will complete everything. Together in the Trinity (Father, Son, Holy Spirit), God will restore all that's been stolen and lost. The once pristine community between God and humanity and of humanity toward humanity will be as it should be—full of harmony and *shalom*.

We began the Bible ninety days ago with God as Creator—and we end with grace. "May the grace of the Lord Jesus be with God's holy people" (Revelation 22:21). Amen!

Lord, thank you for sustaining me through this rapid reading of the Bible. Would you bring to mind all I've learned as I live my life for you? Thank you that all will be made well, that you'll order everything aright. Help me live in light of the New Heavens and the New Earth! Amen!

CONCLUSION

THE STORY OF SCRIPTURE

Congratulations on reading the entire Bible in ninety days! I'm sure there were moments when you felt you could not do it. But here you are, having completed a read-through from Genesis to Revelation. We began in chaos, then creation. A garden housed the first humans who experienced radical fellowship with the One who created them. Even before they fell into temptation, God had a plan to redeem them.

One bite of a piece of forbidden fruit, and further chaos ensued, followed by death and the reign of sin. Banished from the garden, humanity had to eke out an existence without the constant fellowship of their Creator. But God, in his infinite wisdom, found people to bless and lead. He saved humanity through the flood. He chose Abraham, Isaac, and Jacob, who would become the building blocks of the nation of Israel. Through Joseph (Israel's son), he protected this fledgling nation from starvation, using even the betrayal of brothers for the betterment of his people.

When Israel groaned under slavery, God raised up Moses to deliver them. He gave the Law to Moses to help govern and rein in the people (and show their need for a savior, because they could not measure up in their own strength). He enacted the sacrificial system to atone for the sins of humanity—with a tabernacle and then a temple as the center of worship. He raised up a lineage of priests to serve both God and the people.

God empowered Joshua to conquer a land (Canaan), warning the people not to intermarry or chase after idols. Very specifically, God cautioned the people of Israel to follow only God, or they would suffer exile.

To govern the wayward people, God raised up judges, then kings, culminating in the reign of David, whose bloodline would bring a messiah to the people. The nation divided into a northern kingdom (tending toward idolatry) and a southern kingdom near Jerusalem (where the temple stood). Even so, every one of the judges and kings failed God in some way. God sent prophets to correct the leaders and the nation, but often the people rebelled, which ultimately resulted in their exile to Babylon. Eventually they returned and rebuilt the temple (though not as glorious as the one built by King David's son Solomon). In the intertestamental period, God fell silent, and the world waited.

God, who had been far off, came near. He is said to have pitched his tent on earth in the person of Jesus Christ, who was born of a virgin in the town of Bethlehem, the lineage of King David coursing through his veins. Where humankind failed, Jesus never did. He lived a perfect, sinless life, and he set people free from demonic oppression, health issues, and their sin-infused lifestyles. He frustrated the religious elite. He poured his life into a group of people called disciples. He fed people, walked on water, and raised the dead to life. He taught as one who had authority, and he loved those on the outskirts of life. He presented the kingdom of God as near, available, and wholly upside-down.

Jesus chose to die on a cross, embodying the entire sacrificial system. He died once for all, taking the sin of humanity upon himself, providing a way for us to know God as Father. The veil in the temple that prevented fellowship between a holy God and a sinful people was rent in two, ushering us into the holy of holies, the very presence of God. Jesus conquered death, sin, and the enemy of our souls, Satan, rendering him a defeated foe. The grave could not hold the Author of life. Jesus resurrected on the third day, having been dead and entombed. He appeared to Mary of Magdala, then to his disciples, then to five hundred others before ascending to the Father, where he sits now at the right hand of the throne of God, ever living to intercede for us.

He sent the Holy Spirit to the people of God, inaugurating the church. He rescued Saul, remaking him into Paul the apostle, who wrote many letters to instruct the embryonic church. We are now living in this age of grace, forgiven of our sins (because of Jesus), building the kingdom of God (what a privilege!), and waiting for the return of Jesus to set everything right. We live in the tension of the now and the not yet, in an unfinished story.

The future is bright! The story has a happily ever after for the follower of Jesus. We are set free to bring freedom, healed to be healers, redeemed to become ministers of reconciliation. What a privilege it is to be known by God and to be part of his plan!

I pray that this foray into reading the Bible rapidly has expanded your heart and mind to see yourself in the story of Scripture. I pray you have deeper insight into the plan of God and his counterintuitive ways. I pray you have fallen more in love with the God who chases after his people, who sacrifices himself for their well-being, and who pours affection on those he loves. May this ninety-day adventure bring you a deeper love for the Word of God, and may the words of God's beautiful book inform the way you live before him in joy.

ACKNOWLEDGMENTS

Thank you to the team at Bethany House who championed this book from its infancy. Andy McGuire, you gave me permission to do what my heart wanted, to write about my passion for the Word of God. Jennifer Dukes Lee, you shaped this manuscript into a friendly guide for those who want to know and love the Bible. Sharon Hodge, I appreciate your editorial mind and theological prowess! My experience with the Bethany team has been one of the best of my career—and for that, I am truly grateful. I'm also thankful for agent Cynthia Ruchti, who encouraged this project.

My prayer team, the Writing Prayer Circle, prays me through every manuscript. Huge thanks to Jenny, Amy, Avril, Melissa, Kathy, Tabea, Roblee, Sabrina, Susan, Misty, Rebecca C., Patti, Cheryl, Misti, Aldyth, Ally, Amy, Elaine, Dusty, Paula, Kendra, Boz, Cristin, Yanci, Paul, Brandilyn, Richard, Sue, Christy, Alice, Susie, TJ, Dorian, Darren and Holly, Colette, Patricia, Cheri, Gina, Jessica, Michelle, Denise, Ellen, Lacy, Rebecca J., Lisa, Heidi, Becky, Lea Ann, Michelle W., Julie, Kristin, Becky, Sabina, Anna, Leslie, Tosca, Sophie, Diane, Nicole, Jody, Tim, Susan W., Sandi, Cheryl, Randy, Patrick, Holly, Cyndi, Katy O., Katy G., Judy M., Erin, Jeanne, D'Ann, Liz, Caroline, Anita, Ralph, and Hope. Where would I be without you? Your prayers mean the world to me.

I am deeply indebted to my husband, Patrick, who is, in a way, a ghostwriter of this book. Our theological discussions on daily walks informed my understanding of the grand narrative of Scripture. His theological mind has deeply influenced my own love for the Word of God and all its poetic nuance.

Jesus, you are the reason I write. It's my sincere prayer that you'll use this book to bring biblical literacy to many, as well as deep-seated transformation. I love you with all my heart!

NOTES

Contents

1. This order of the reading partially relies on the one found here from The Bible Project: https://s3-us-west-2.amazonaws.com/tbp-web/media/Quarterlies _Other%20Downloads/RS_Reading%20Plan_1YR.pdf. I changed the rapidity of the reading and added Psalms in a different way.

Day 3: God Creates Families

1. The translator of the *New American Standard Bible* uses the word *contended* in Genesis 32:28.

Day 8: God Loves Our Offerings

1. For a broader explanation, please see John W. Ritenbaugh, "The Offerings of Leviticus (Part Four): The Peace Offering," Church of the Great God, June 2003, https://www.cgg.org/index.cfm/library/article/id/809/the-offerings-of-leviticus -part-four-peace-offering.htm.

Day 14: God Wants Us to Remember and Obey

1. "What Does the Word 'Manna' Mean in Hebrew?," Hebrewversity, https:// www.hebrewversity.com/word-mannamean-hebrew/.

Day 29: God Rebukes and Encourages

1. J. R. R. Tolkien, *The Tolkien Reader* (New York: Ballentine Books, 1966), 87.

Day 59: God Sends Jesus!

1. Study cited in Aaron Earls, "More Americans Read the Bible During the Pandemic," *Lifeway Research*, October 21, 2021, https://research.lifeway.com /2021/10/21/more-americans-read-the-bible-during-the-pandemic/.

Day 85: God Empowers Perseverance and Patience

1. "Pistis," New Testament Greek Lexicon–NAS, Bible Study Tools, https:// www.biblestudytools.com/lexicons/greek/nas/pistis.html.

Mary DeMuth is a literary agent, international speaker, and podcaster, as well as a novelist and nonfiction author of over forty books, including *Love, Pray, Listen* (Bethany House 2022). She loves to help people restory their lives. She lives in Texas with her husband of thirty-three years and is mom to three adult children. Find out more at marydemuth.com. Be prayed for on her daily prayer podcast with over 4 million downloads: marydemuth.com/prayeveryday. For sexual abuse resources, visit wetoo.org. For cards, prints, and artsy fun, go to marydemuth.com/art.